PRACTICAL EVERYDAY
with Audio CD

by Steven Collins

This is the best book on conversational English
and phrasal verbs I've ever read. When I'm
in the UK, I never go anywhere without it.

Hideki Noda
(celebrated Japanese playwright)

ISBN 0-9528358-2-7
978-0-9528358-2-0

www.learnenglishadvanced.com

Montserrat Publishing

MONTSERRAT PUBLISHING

First edition 1996
First edition with CD 2007
Second edition 2009
Third edition 2009 (autumn)
Fourth edition 2010
Fifth edition 2012
Sixth edition 2013

Montserrat Publishing
5 Coverdale Road
London
NW2 4DB
England
Tel/Fax: 004420 8909 1247

Illustrations:
Alex Stead
www.alexsteadart.com
info@alexsteadart.com

Typesetting & Cover Design:
Peter Sjöstedt Hughes

www.learnenglishadvanced.com

To my Sofie-Sofe, La Princesa

Steven Collins was born in London in 1960. He grew up in Harrow and qualified as a lawyer (solicitor) in 1987, having done a Master's in Law at Trinity Hall, Cambridge. He then decided to make a complete change of career and went into T.E.F.L. (Teaching English as a Foreign Language). Having lived and taught in Italy and Spain, he returned to London in 1993 to write this book and to open his own school in Central London, specialising in practical English for advanced students. However, in 2008 he retired from teaching to concentrate full time on writing and publishing.

Book Two

Advanced Everyday English with audio CD

By Steven Collins

Available at all good bookshops and online stores including Amazon

Advanced Everyday English is an updated, extended and improved version of More Practical Everyday English, book 2 in the Practical Everyday English series, which is now out of print.

ISBN 0-9528358-4-3
978-0-9528358-4-4

Book Three

High-level Everyday English with audio CD

By Steven Collins

Available at all good bookshops and online stores including Amazon

High-level Everyday English is book 3 in the Practical Everyday English series, and is designed for students who have reached a very advanced stage in their English studies...but still need a little help with difficult everyday vocabulary.

ISBN 0-9528358-5-1
978-0-9528358-5-1

www.learnenglishadvanced.com

Introduction
PRACTICAL EVERYDAY ENGLISH
Steven Collins

Can you speak English as well as this?:

*Yesterday the Chairman of ABC Ltd, one of Britain's largest companies, said: "The economy cannot **put up with** any more wage increases this year. The strength of the service industry is **overrated** and cannot be relied upon to **make up** for the **appalling** performance of British manufacturers. A change can only **come about** if the Government **gets things underway** immediately, before we plunge even further into recession.*

*Mr Smith, the Managing Director of a small clothing company in the South-West, said: "When I set up my business at the beginning of the year, I did not know **what I was letting myself in for. I took it for granted** that strikes were **unheard of** in this part of the country and interest rates would **keep up with** the rate of inflation, but everything has **turned out** to be less **straightforward".***

Or this?:

At the Post office:

Clerk:	*Hi Mrs. Johnson, I haven't seen you for **ages**. What have you **been up to**?*
Mrs Johnson:	***Bringing up** three screaming kids and **putting up** with a **nagging** husband. **I could** really **do with** a week on my own... and then I could **get down to sorting** myself **out**.*
Clerk:	*I know how you feel. We all need time **to gather** our thoughts and escape from the **relentless** stress of our daily lives.*
Mrs Johnson:	*Oh dear. You sound worse than me.*
Clerk:	*Not really... You should know by now that you must take everything I say with **a pinch of salt**... Now what can I do for you today?*
Mrs Johnson:	*Well, I must **get** these parcels **off** to Australia before Christmas. What's the quickest way?*
Clerk:	*You can send it by Swiftair. It guarantees three day delivery... but it'll **work out** more expensive than the **run of the mill** postal service.*
Mrs Johnson:	*Yes I know, but it has to be done so I **might as well** go for it.*
Clerk:	*Fine…but you'd better **get a move on**. Last post leaves at 12.30.*

I would now like to ask you two further questions:

1. ## Can you understand every single word in these passages?

2. ## Would you be able to use all of them naturally in an everyday conversation?

If the answer to either of these questions is "no", then I believe this book can be of great help to you.

Purpose of the Book

You may feel, as an upper intermediate or advanced student, very frustrated at your recent lack of progress in English. Your grammar is good; you have taken and passed some of the important recognised written English exams but you still struggle to follow a conversation between native English speakers. You feel stupid and depressed that, despite years of studying English and even living in an English speaking country, you keep having to say, "Sorry, I don't understand. Can you repeat that please?" You pick up a newspaper and often only understand 50% of what you are reading, especially reported speech. Television and the cinema, without subtitles, present you with enormous difficulties... Or maybe you can understand nearly everything but feel you cannot express yourself in modern, idiomatic English.

DON'T WORRY. RELAX! THIS IS ALL PERFECTLY NORMAL.
If you study this book one page a day and keep listening to the CD (at the back of the book), you will soon notice a huge improvement in your listening and speaking skills.

The Audio CD (see back of book)
The CD with this book only relates to the dialogues appearing at the end of each chapter. I make no apology for the fact that it is only an audio CD and not a CD Rom with pretty pictures, games and music. You are not children! The biggest problem for adult students of English is understanding Practical Everyday English spoken at speed. (Do you speak your own language slowly?)

It is different from any other English aural teaching aid you will have used before. Most audio work in the English teaching world is presented by trained actors speaking unnaturally slowly. Although this CD has been professionally recorded in a modern studio, the voices are those of a variety of English speakers, all talking at their normal speed. One of the male speakers is particularly fast. This is excellent practice for all students. You are unlikely to be able to understand the CD without the text from the book in front of you. After you have listened to a particular passage while following in the book, you should then listen to it again with the book closed... and again... and again.

This way, you will soon get accustomed to listening to conversational English spoken at high speed.

The Method and Structure of the Book

Practical Everyday English is not just a book, but a **method** which helps upper intermediate and advanced students to understand and then use everyday vocabulary. Most of the material in the book is good conversational English rather than academic. However, I should like to point out that "good conversational English" does *not* mean street slang. There is included within the book a small amount of slang which now passes as "acceptable" English but even members of the British Royal Family would use most of the phrases and idioms contained in these pages.

The method is simple: in almost every example in the book, apart from the first few pages, I have tried to use a word or phrase that has been taught on earlier pages. For example, in Chapter 5 the reader is taught the expression **To get carried away** which means to become too enthusiastic about something. One of the examples given is:

> *I got a bit **carried away** with the shopping today. My wife is **bound** to **hit the roof** when she finds out how much money I've **got through**.*

He or she will already know **To be bound to**, **To hit the roof** and **To get through** because they appear in earlier chapters. Therefore, after reading these words and expressions time and time again, the students will find themselves being able to understand, speak and write Practical Everyday English almost automatically.

The book consists of:
Nine Chapters, each one containing
Three Lessons consisting of ten or more words or expressions, plus examples.
At the end of each chapter is a series of
Dialogues containing words taught in that chapter and finally a 'gap-filling'
Exercise, with answers at the end of the book. And an
Audio CD containing all the dialogues.

For Students
Suggestions on How to Use the Book as a Self-Study Guide

There are basically two ways in which you can use this book:

First Method

You can study the book by reading each lesson as it appears (i.e. from Page One, Chapter One). It is probably sufficient to study one lesson a week and then go back and revise each chapter as it is finished. After finishing each chapter, you should read through the dialogues while listening to the CD and test yourself by completing the exercises.

The help of a native English speaking teacher would be of great benefit as you can think of your own examples which can then be corrected by this person. However, the book is specifically designed for self-study and, providing you have the required level of vocabulary and grammar, 'outside' help should not prove necessary.

Second Method

The second method may be preferred by those of you who have little time to sit down and study the book thoroughly. At the back of the book you will see an index of all the words and expressions included, together with the page numbers.

In other words, the book can be used almost like a dictionary. If, whilst reading or listening to English, you find a word or expression you have never heard before or perhaps you have heard but do not know how to use, then try to find it in the index. This will refer to the particular word or expression and generally to two or more examples. However, it is quite possible that you will not understand some of the examples because, as mentioned earlier, they nearly all contain words from previous lessons which you may not have studied before.

Therefore, if you have time to study, you should adopt the first method. Once you feel confident, you should try to use what you have learned at every available opportunity.

For Teachers
Suggestions on How to Teach Small Classes Using this Book

Firstly, I have to be honest and tell you that, even though you do not have to be a native English speaker in order to teach properly from this book, your own conversational and grammatical English should be native speaker level; near native level is not sufficient. As an English mother tongue speaker teaching from this book for many years, I have often had to say to a student, "Your example is grammatically correct... but we just wouldn't say it like that". Only a native level speaker can say that to a class. In addition, a good few years' experience of teaching high level students will also be invaluable.

PREPARATION

Step One
The first thing you must do is familiarise yourself with the text. This does not mean reading the book word-for-word but simply getting to grips with the general layout of the chapters and the philosophy behind the method.

Step Two
This book contains a wide range of formal and informal vocabulary which is essential for the advanced level learner of English. The material is presented by way of practical examples which usually contain words which the student will have studied at an earlier stage in the book. The important thing for you to do at this stage is to ask yourself: "Are my students ready for this level of English?" There is no point in teaching someone, for example, the difference between **To make a fuss** and **To make a fuss** *of* (see Page 3) or complicated phrasal verbs such as **To come over** (Page 12), if they cannot construct or understand basic English sentences.

Step Three
If the sudents are 'up to it', they should have a copy of the book which they should not bring to class. They ought also to be told not to look ahead at the words they are going to study in the lesson but only use the book at home for revision purposes.

IN THE LESSON

Step One
You should begin by asking the students if they know the meaning of the words or expressions you are going to teach them from the book. For argument's sake, let us take the very first lesson; we begin with the words **Quite a few**. Most students think that this means 'not many'. It is important not to tell them what it means but to encourage them to work it out for themselves, which is why it is mentioned earlier that the students should not read ahead. This is best done by reading the first example to them. They should then be able to guess the meaning of the word. Whether or not they have been able to do this, you should then read the second example.

Step Two

Once the students have heard both examples (sometimes there are three or four) and worked out the sense of the word, you should then explain it in more detail, referring to the meaning given in the book.

It is then a good idea to ask one of the students to explain the meaning of the example. In this way, the students will begin to feel that they completely understand a word that they were unsure of or had not heard previously.

Step Three

You should continue in exactly the same way until that lesson finishes; that is, introducing a word, giving examples, asking students what they think the word means and finally giving a more complete explanation. At the end of the lesson, you should record where you finish. For example, imagine you finish the lesson with the word **Fussy**, then you should make the following record in your notebook:

> [Date] – **Quite a few** *(Page 1)* ... **Fussy** *(Page 3)*

Step Four

For homework, you should ask the students to study everything you have done that day, at home, by referring to the book. They should then prepare their own examples for the next lesson.

Step Five

At the beginning of the following lesson, you should go around the class asking for examples and explanations of the words you taught in the previous lesson. In the first few lessons, it is important to encourage the students to use simple constructions. You will find that the majority of the mistakes they make will be grammatcal. Once again, it is important to encourage them to think and correct themselves. If they have used the word or expression more or less correctly but have got the tense wrong, then instead of correcting them, you should simply ask them: "What tense should you be using?" In this way, their grammar will improve as well as their vocabulary.

Step Six

Some complicated constructions have been used in the examples. If, for example, you discover that your students do not know the tenses we use after the verb **To wish** (e.g. the past continuous – "I wish I wasn't going out tonight"), then it may be a good idea to stop the lesson at that point and go through the grammatical problems with them (but their grammar should already be very good and you should not waste too much time).

Step Seven

After they have studied the first two lessons of Chapter One, you should encourage them to use the words they have learned, when giving their own examples. Many of the examples included in this book have been provided by students themselves. When a student was once asked to give an example of **To wind up** (see Page 148), he said "If you don't cut out smoking, you could **wind up** having to undergo heart surgery". He had already studied **To cut out** and **To undergo** in previous lessons.

Step Eight

Finally, the importance of revision must be emphasised. As mentioned earlier, in nearly all the examples, the words which are used have been previously taught so the students will automatically be doing some sort of revision all the time. However, this is not sufficient; they need to be able to give you examples 'on the spur of the moment'.

Therefore, it is suggested each time you finish a chapter, you should go back and revise that chapter by insisting that all students close their exercise books, look up and respond quickly when asked for examples. You should then ask them to read at home the dialogues appearing at the end of the chapter whilst listening to the CD and then get them to complete the gap-filling exercise. Every time you finish three chapters, you should do a revision of those last three chapters in the same 'quick fire' way. Lastly, when Chapter Nine is finished, a complete revision of the book should be done. By constant revision, you will notice that the students become much more natural in their use of Practical Everyday English.

If you follow the procedures as set out above (there are of course no rules – this is only a guideline), and the students are at the right level, you should derive much pleasure from teaching your students this level of English, especially when you can see that, at long last, they are beginning to 'get the hang of' this rich but mind-boggling language.

Steven Collins
London 2006

Website: www.learnenglishadvanced.com

Lesson One

Quite a few – Quite a number of (Quite a lot)

Examples:
- *We've got **quite a few** Americans working here.*
- *I'd like to order another one hundred boxes of red wine; we sold **quite a number of** them last summer.*

It should be noted that **Quite a few** is used for countable nouns only, whilst for uncountable nouns one could use Quite a bit of:

e.g.   1.   *They had **quite a bit of** money in their Clients' Account.*
       2.   *Don't worry, there's **quite a bit of** time left yet.*

Quite a bit (and Quite a lot) can also mean **quite often**:

e.g.   *I've been to Japan **quite a bit** this year.*

Also note the use of Quite a while which means for **quite a long time**,

e.g.   1.   *I've been studying English for **quite a while** now.*
       2.   *A: How long are you intending to stay here?*
            *B: I'm not sure but probably **quite a while**.*

Ages (A very long time)

Examples:
- *I meet your brother quite a bit these days but I haven't seen your sister in/for* **ages**.*
- *It seems **ages** since I was last here.*

* **In** would only be used after a negative or superlative construction,

e.g.   *It's the **best** film I've seen **in** ages.*

But not in the future, i.e. we would **not** say: *We won't arrive **in** ages.*

Well off (Rich)

Examples:
- *He is so **well off**, he doesn't know what to spend his money on.*
- *If I were as **well off** as she is, I'd retire.*

Well off does not necessarily have to refer to money; it can also be used in respect of opportunities, facilities etc.,

e.g.   *Young people today don't know how **well off** they are.*

i.e.   children nowadays do not appreciate the opportunities which are open to them and which were not available to their parents.

Better off is the comparative form of Well off, i.e. **richer**.

e.g.   *He is far **better off** than I am.*

However, it can also be used to mean "It would be/it is better for you, him, it, etc.",

e.g.   1.   *You'd be **better off** going on the motorway than taking a country route, if you want to arrive there by 6 o'clock.*

        2.   *She's better off without her husband; he made her life a misery.*

Note that this meaning of **Better off** is still used in the comparative sense. This construction should not be confused with Had better which is a slightly stronger form of **should**,

e.g.   *I'd **better** go now; I've got quite a few things to do.*

The opposite of Better off is Worse off, i.e. **poorer**.

e.g.   *Even though my brother has been working for quite a number of years, he is **worse off** than me.*

To hear of (To be familiar with/to know the existence of/to recognise the name of a person, thing or situation – usually famous in a particular field of entertainment, art or profession)

Examples:
- *Have you ever **heard of** a company called ABC Limited?*
- *I'm surprised you've never **heard of** him; he's quite well-off.*
- *Before we came to London, we had never **heard of** this type of crime.**

To hear and To hear of, therefore, have different meanings and it is quite possible **to hear of** a musician without ever having **heard** him or her play.

* i.e. *We never knew that this type of crime occurred.*

To hear about

    i.   (To hear, find out what has happened to someone)

Example:
-     A: *Have you **heard about** John?*
-     B: *No, tell me.*
-     A: *Unfortunately he has lost his job.*

    ii.   (To find out about something)

Examples:
- *I found this school in the Yellow Pages. How did you **hear about/of*** it?*
- *I was very happy to **hear about/of*** the recent addition to your family.*

* Note that To hear of can be used in the same way as **To hear about** for this meaning only.

    iii.   (To receive information about someone/something from somebody else – e.g. reputation, character etc.)

Examples:
- *At long last we have met; I've **heard** quite a bit **about** you.*
- *I'm surprised you haven't **heard** more **about** our company; we've got quite a reputation.**

*There is a slight difference between the above sentence and "I'm surprised you haven't **heard of** that company......" which means that the person being spoken to does not know that the company exists.
The sentence above (**about**), on the other hand, suggests that the person is aware of the company's existence but knows nothing more about it.

To hear from (To receive news, communication from someone)

Examples:
- *I haven't **heard from** him in ages.*
- A: *When was the last time you **heard from** your daughter?*
- B: *Oh, quite a while ago.*

Fussy (Difficult to please, not easily satisfied)

Examples:
- *Tell me what you want to eat before I make dinner because I know you're a **fussy** eater/how **fussy** you are.*
- *She's not very **fussy** about whom she goes out with, providing he's well-off.*

Note also the words Choosy, Particular and Picky which have the same meaning as **Fussy**.

To make a fuss (To complain, to be difficult, i.e. a person, not a thing)

Examples:
- *If I'm in a restaurant and the service is slow, I can't help making a **fuss**.*
- *I do wish you'd stop making a **fuss** and continue with your work.*

Do not confuse this expression with To make a fuss of / To fuss over which means to show affection towards a person or animal, to give someone a lot of care and attention.
e.g.
1. *My dog loves to **be made a fuss of**/fussed over.*
2. *We've stayed in quite a few hotels recently where the staff **made** too much **fuss of** us.*

Stale (Unfresh – e.g. bread, biscuits or air)

Examples:
- *In a restaurant:*
  *Waiter, sorry to make a fuss, but this bread is **stale**.*
- *I think I'd better open the window in the conference room; it's a bit **stale*** in there.*
- *Can you remind me of how the company's accounts system works? I am sorry, my mind is a little **stale** on this matter.°*

Note the word Stalemate which describes the situation where neither side in a dispute or negotiations can progress or win,
e.g. *It's clear that we've reached a **stalemate**; we'd be better off starting again.*
*The word Stuffy is probably more common as far as air is concerned.
° i.e. I have forgotten how it works.*

3

To go off

i. (To go bad – food/milk)
Examples:
- *This milk smells like it has **gone off**/it's **off**.*
- *Don't be so fussy! I'm sure those sausages haven't **gone off**/aren't **off**.*

ii. (To ring – alarm clock/bell)

Examples:
- *My alarm clock **went off** an hour earlier than it was supposed to this morning.*
- *You'd be better off without a car alarm; they're always **going off** at the wrong time.*

Note that **To go off** can only be used for an alarm and not, for example, for the telephone or a doorbell. One could, however, say *I wasn't happy when the phone **went** at six o'clock this morning.*

iii. (To explode, to fire, i.e. a bomb or a gun)

Examples:
- *Have you heard about that bomb which **went off** in the city centre yesterday?*
- *He claims that the gun **went off** accidentally, but I've heard about his past and I'm a bit suspicious.*

iv. (To stop liking something or someone) **Colloquial**

Examples:
- *I've **gone off** her coffee. I think we'd all be better off if she just offered us tea.*
- *She **went off** her last boyfriend after hearing about his past relationships.*
- *I'm **going off** the idea* of doing business with them, they're far too fussy!*

* i.e. *I'm changing my mind about ....*

v. (To be sent – a letter or a fax – often used in the office)

Example:
- *Quite a number of letters **went off** this morning but they won't arrive for ages because of the strike.*

vi.   (To leave for a particular place, to travel around)

         Examples:
-      On the telephone:
  *I'm sorry, you've missed her; she **went (off)** to work quite a while ago.*
- *I heard about your journey; you **went (off)** round the world, didn't you?*

vii.   (To be switched off/to stop working – usually something powered by electricity or gas)

         Example:
- *This room smells stale because the air conditioning **went off** during the night.**

* Compare with *...the air conditioning **is** off,* which means that it was not switched on in the first place.

To get one's own back on someone/To get someone back (To get one's revenge)

         Examples:
- *It's no use making a fuss of him. He still wants to **get his own back on you/to get you back** for what you did to him last week.*
- *I've heard that the bomb which went off near the police station was planted by a terrorist organisation, trying to get **their own back** for recent arrests.*

Compare with To get/come back to someone on/with something which means to come back to someone **on** a particular matter or **with** the information they require. It is usually used on the telephone,

   e.g.   1.   *I'm sorry I don't have the details **on** me now. Would you mind if I **got/came back to you** later (on that matter)?*

           2.   *Can you **get/come back to me with** their phone number this afternoon; I want to make a fuss about the stale food they sent us.*

May/Might as well

i.   (One should do something only because there is nothing better to do)

         Examples:
- *We **may as well** go to John's place again, unless you can think of something more interesting to do.*
- A: *Shall we go off to work now?:*

        B: *I suppose we **might as well**.*

Might as well and May as well are interchangeable, but it is very important to understand the difference between May/Might as well and May/Might. The difference between *We may/might go to the pub* and *We may/might as well go to the pub* is that the first sentence expresses a **possibility** – *Maybe we won't go,* whilst the second sentence expresses a **suggestion** to go to the pub, but only because there is nothing better to do. This meaning of **May as well,** therefore, has a negative feel about it.

5

ii. (There is no harm in/it's worthwhile doing something)

    Examples:
- A: *Do you think I should take a pullover with me to Greece?*
- B: *Well you probably won't need it but you **might as well** take it just in case.*
- *Even though I've got quite a number of dictionaries at home, I **might as well** buy this one as it's so cheap.*

i.e. *You will lose nothing so therefore it's worth doing.*

iii. (It would be the same/it wouldn't make any difference, so therefore one should do the easier or cheaper thing)

    Examples:
- *As the weather is so hot and sunny this year, I've gone off the idea of going abroad; I **may as well** stay in England.*
- *The office party was so boring, I **might as well** have remained* at home.*

This form of **Might as well** is generally used where one has a choice of two or more things which are of similar quality and, because of this, one should choose the most convenient one.
* Note that the past of I **might/may as well** is I **may/might as well have** [+ past participle].

To do up

i. (To tie up, button up, fasten, e.g. zip)

    Examples:
- *I don't want to make a fuss, but you'd better **do** your shirt **up** before meeting the boss.*
- A: *Do you want me to give you a hand in **doing up** your dress?*
- B: *Yes, you may as well.*

The opposite of **To do up** is To undo,
    e.g.   1.   *Would you mind if I **undid** my jacket?*
                2.   *Your shoelaces are **undone**!*

ii. (To decorate, renovate)

Examples:
- *If we don't go away this summer, we might as well **do** the house **up**.*
- *It's been ages since we last had our house **done up**.*

*"I don't want to make a fuss, but you'd better **do** your shirt **up** before meeting the boss."*

(see Page 6)

Lesson Two

To take after (To be similar to an elder member of the same family – usually in character rather than in appearance)

Examples:
- My daughter likes to be made a fuss of; she **takes after** me in that respect.
- You **take after** your grandfather; he also used to go off people quickly.

To bet (to be almost certain something will or will not happen) **Colloquial**

Examples:
- I **bet** you won't be able to do up the bathroom yourself.
- A: He says that he'll be better off than all of us in a few years.
  B: I wouldn't **bet on** it!

The literal meaning of the verb To bet is to put money on something happening; e.g. the winner of a race, competition or a match,

  e.g. I bet £10 **on** Liverpool winning the cup this year.

Also note the informal expression Do you want a bet? which means that the speaker is challenging something someone else has just said,

  e.g. A. I'll get my own back on you one day
  B. **Do you want a bet?**

What's the point? (What's the use/purpose, what for?)

Examples:
- **What's the point in/of** coming to England, if you don't want to meet English people? You may as well stay in your own country.
- A: Shall we employ another Accounts Clerk?
  B: **What's the point**? We've already got quite a few.

We can also use Point in a negative form with There is i.e. "It's useless, a waste of time",

  e.g. **There's no point (in)** speaking to him; he takes after his father, in that he never listens to anything anyone says.

Also be careful not to confuse this expression with What's the point you are trying to make? which means, What are you trying to say?

To tread (To step on something)

Examples:
- When I was in the army, I had to be careful not **to tread** on unexploded bombs in case they went off.
- You've just **trodden on** my clean floor with your dirty shoes. I'll get you back for this!

The paradigm of **To tread** is "tread, trod, trodden" and is always followed by the preposition **on** unless it is a liquid or something like a liquid, in which case **in** must be used,

    e.g.   *Some children enjoy **treading in** puddles after it has been raining.*

Also note that To tread can be used in a figurative sense with people, meaning to treat people as though they do not matter;

    e.g.   *Just because she is well-off, she thinks she can **tread on** everyone.*

This meaning of **To tread** is only used to describe a person's general attitude or character towards others and not for an action against one person. For example, one would **not** say *She trod on me yesterday.*

Overdraft, To be/go overdrawn (An agreement with a bank to be able to withdraw money in excess of one's account, to withdraw more money from the bank than one has in one's account)

Examples:
- Instead of relying on your **overdraft** facility, you'd be better off taking out a loan.
- I bet she won't be able to clear her **overdraft** by the end of the year.*
- Letter from a bank:
  Dear Mr Smith,
  It has come to our attention that your account
  is **overdrawn**° in the sum of £200[†].

* i.e. *I'm sure she won't be able to pay back the money she owes the bank.*
° Note that in conversation, it is more common to say *I'm overdrawn* than *My account is overdrawn.*
† The phrase In the sum of is very often used in formal letters concerning money. In spoken English, one would normally use **by**.

To look forward to (To wait with pleasure)

Examples:
- I was really **looking forward to** seeing* Alice;
  I hadn't heard from her in ages.
- A: We're going to start doing up our new house next week.
  B: Are you **looking forward to** it?*
- I'm not **looking forward to**° receiving my bank statement;
  I must be overdrawn by at least £500.

* This expression is extremely common in written and spoken English. In the final paragraph of a letter, either formal or informal, we often write, *I look forward to hearing from you soon.* It is important to note the irregular construction, i.e. "**Look forward to + gerund**" (**not infinitive**) or we can simply use a noun or **it**,

> e.g.   *I am looking forward to* **Christmas/it.**

One should also be careful not to make the common mistake of confusing *To look* **forward** *to* with *To look for* which means to search for;

> e.g.   *I'm* **looking for** *my glasses. I hope no one has trodden on them.*

° Note that when *Look Forward To* is used in the negative, it still means the event **is** going to happen (i.e. the bank statement is definitely going to arrive) but the speaker is **not** happy about it.

> e.g.   *I'm not* **looking forward to** *going out tonight.*

This means the person **is** going out, but would rather not.

Day off (A day's holiday)

> Examples:
> - *Can we get back to you tomorrow? The person dealing with this matter has got the* **day off** *today.*
> - *I have two extra* **days off** *next month. I'm really looking forward to them!*

Do not confuse **Day off** with *Off-day* which means a bad day or a day in which one does not perform as well as one usually does,

> e.g.   1.   *I would have bet a million pounds on her passing her exams but she failed. She must have had an* **off-day**.
>   2.   *The captain of the football team is having an* **off-day***; he might as well not have played!*

One should also note that **Off-day** can only be used with the auxiliary verb **To have**, i.e. one cannot say *It's an off-day*.

Finally, one should note that although people often use a *week off*, a *month off* or a *year off*, etc. *Off-week* and *Off-month* are not so common.

To show off (To show that one is very proud of one's abilities, achievements or possessions, to boast)

> Examples:
> - *I don't want to* **show off** *but I must tell you that I came first in all my exams when I was at university.*
> - One tennis player to another:
>   *Just because I'm having an off-day today, (it) doesn't mean you have to* **show off** *in front of everyone watching.*
> - *It's surprising his friends haven't gone off him, after the way* he keeps* **showing off** *his new car.*

Show-off can also be used as a noun, i.e. a person who shows off,

> e.g.   *I am looking forward to getting my own back on that* **show-off**.

We can also say that someone is a *big-head* (noun) or that he or she is *big-headed* (adjective).

* Note that *After the way* means considering, as a consequence of. It very often follows *It is (not) surprising*.

10

Posh (Upper class, sophisticated) **Colloquial**

Examples:
- *There's no point (in) speaking with a **posh** accent; they can tell where you really come from.*
- *You can undo your jacket. This restaurant isn't <u>that</u>* **posh**.*

* If **that** is stressed, it means the restaurant is **posh**, but not as much as the person thinks. If, on the other hand, **that** is not stressed, it means the restaurant is not **posh** at all.

Turnover

i. (The total amount of money/income that a business receives during a certain period of time)

Examples:
- *A **turnover** of a million pounds should help to clear our overdraft.*
- *Have you heard them showing off about how much their **turnover** has increased this year?*

Note that the profit of a company is its turnover less its expenses.

ii. (The speed, rate at which staff* join and leave a company/business etc.)

Examples:
- *The company has such a high **turnover** of staff° that I hardly recognise anyone from week to week.*
- *I've gone off the idea of spending more money on advertising for new employees. What we really need to do is reduce our **turnover** of staff.*

* Note that one could have a high **turnover** of students at a school, meaning that there is a constant flow of **students**.
° i.e. *There are so many people coming and going.*

*"There's no point in speaking with a **posh** accent; they can tell where you really come from."*

Lesson Three

To cope with (To be able to tolerate, manage, bear a situation or person)

Examples:
- *Sometimes I think I'd be better off without a job:*
  *I can't **cope with** this one any longer.*
- *I'm really looking forward to my parents going away.*
  *I can hardly **cope with** them at the moment.*

Note the verb To handle which has the same meaning as **To cope with** but is also used to express the idea of dealing with something or someone,

e.g.
1. *I've got the day off tomorrow. Would you mind **handling** this matter?*
2. *It's OK, I'll **handle** Mr Jones – I'm dying to get my own back on him.*

To handle is probably more colloquial than **To cope with**. One should also note that **To handle** always requires an object. This is not necessarily the case with **To cope with**, although the preposition **with** is dropped.

e.g.
1. *How is he **coping**?*
2. *I can't **cope**.*
3. *How is he **handling it**?*
4. *I can't **handle it**.*

To come/go over

i. (To come/go to someone's house) **Colloquial**

Examples:
- *Would you like to **come over*** tomorrow, as you've got the day off?*
- *I'm **going over** to Peter's* tonight to help him do up his bathroom.*

* Note that it is not necessary to mention the word **house**.

ii. (To visit from abroad the country where the speaker is situated –
To come over, to visit another country for a specific purpose –
To go over*)

Examples:
- *My wife's parents are **coming over** from France for a month.*
  I don't think I'll be able to cope!
- *I'm really looking forward to you **coming over** and seeing me.*
- *We heard about your trip. Didn't you **go over** to see your son in Italy?*

* Note that To go over (not **To come over**) also means to revise, check, explain/discuss,

e.g.
1. *I'm not looking forward to **going over** that subject again with them.*
   We always end up arguing.
2. *I'll get back to you tomorrow and we can **go over** it together.*

iii. (To happen to someone, to make someone do or say something strange or out of character – generally used with *I don't know what* or *I wonder what*)*

Examples:
- A: *Just because you've gone off him, there's no need to behave like that.*
  B: *Yes you're right – I don't know what **came over** me.*
- *It's most unusual for my son to call me three times in the same week; I wonder what has **come over** him.*

iv. (To give a certain impression – generally the first one – i.e. a person or what a person says)*

Examples:
- *He **comes over** as a real show-off but actually he's quite shy.*
- *I know you didn't mean to sound ungrateful, but that's how it **came over** to us.*

v. (To be successfully communicated, understood – e.g. a message, idea, speech or way of expressing oneself)*

Examples:
- *I could understand what he was saying about the company's turnover, but I don't know if it **came over** to the other Directors.*
- *I've been going off him recently and besides, his style of humour doesn't really **come over** very well on television.*

* Note that only **To come over** and *not* **To go over** can be used for these three meanings. However, To come across has the same meanings as **iv.** and **v.** above.

To come round (To wake up* after an operation or fainting, to regain consciousness)°

Examples:
- *We might as well stay at home instead of going to the hospital. He still hasn't **come round** (from the operation).*
- *I couldn't handle the heat yesterday and I fainted but I soon **came round** again.*

To come/go round can be used interchangeably with **To come/go over** to mean to come or to go to someone's house (see Page 12).

* To **come round** does *not* mean to recover. This is something that one would hope to do in the week following the operation – *after* one has **come round**.

° Note that To come to has the same meaning as **To come round** in this sense only.

To come round to (To agree with something eventually – often after a lot of persuasion, to accept the idea of something when it can be seen that there is no alternative)

Examples:
- *The other partners don't agree with our plan at the moment but when they see how much turnover we are losing, I'm sure they'll **come round to** it.*
- *She can't cope with the thought of moving so soon after her husband's death, but give her a couple of months and she'll almost certainly **come round to** the idea.*

To ask/have round/over

i. (To invite to one's house) **Colloquial**

Examples:
- *I used to like her friends but now I've gone off the idea of **asking/having them round**.*
- *I'm sorry the place is in a mess, but we **asked/had** some friends **over** last night.*

To have is generally not used in the imperative, i.e. it would be more common to say *Ask him round tonight!* Also note the possible difference between *I asked them round/over last night* and *I had them over/round last night*. The first sentence does not tell us whether or not the people actually came, only that they were invited. The second sentence, however, assures us that not only were the people invited but they did actually come. In the second example above, we know the people came because the place was in a mess.

ii. (To ask for information, to enquire about something from various people)

Examples:
- *I don't know if what you're saying will come over very well to my colleagues but I'll **ask round** (the office) just in case anyone is interested in attending your conference.*
- *Can you **ask round** (your circle of friends) to see if there's any accommodation available? It doesn't have to be anything too posh.*

Note that only **To ask round** can be used for this meaning and *not* **To ask over** or **To have round/over**.

Reluctant (Unwilling, unhappy about doing something)

Examples:
- *After the way he behaved, I'm **reluctant** to ask him round again.*
- *I'll try to get back to you on it tomorrow but I must warn you that the boss is **reluctant** to let us give out information over the phone.*

14

Note the difference between *I was reluctant to go to the party* and *I reluctantly went to the party*. The first sentence means the person did not want to go to the party, but we do not know whether or not he actually went. *I reluctantly went to the party* tells us for sure that the person attended the party, even though he had no desire to do so.

To turn up

i. (To increase the volume, power)

Examples:
- *What's the point of **turning up** the radio?*
  You're not listening to it anyway.
- *Can you **turn up** the heating please?*
  I take after my mother, in that I'm always cold.

ii. (To arrive/come)

Examples:
- *I'm sorry I didn't **turn up** yesterday but*
  I had to go over to my brother's.
- *Thanks for asking us round.*
  *What time do you want us to **turn up**?*

iii. (To appear – often something/someone which has been lost or is difficult to find)

Examples:
- *A: Has your watch **turned up** yet?*
  B: No, I think I left it on the train. I don't know what came over me.
- *I know you've been looking for a job for ages now, but don't worry,*
  *I'm sure something will **turn up**.*

Remember, it is the lost object that does the **turning up** and not the person looking for it. Therefore, one *cannot* say *I **turned up** my pen yesterday*, but *My pen **turned up** yesterday*.
Also note the word Upturn which means a positive change, an improvement, usually in business or the economy of a country,
    e.g. *The Minister was reluctant to admit that an **upturn** in trade was not likely in the near future.*

A turn-up for the books (A great surprise)

Examples:
- *I couldn't believe it when I heard about his appointment as*
  *Managing Director. What a **turn-up for the books**!*
- *After making a fuss for so long, it was a real **turn-up for the books***
  for my mother-in-law to agree to come over from Italy to see us.

To turn down

i. (To decrease the volume, power)

Examples:

- *Can you please **turn** the stereo **down**? I can't cope with all that noise.*
- *There's no point in **turning** the air conditioning **down**; you might as well turn it off.*

Note To keep down would be used for voices and noise.

e.g. ***Keep** your voices **down**. This is a very posh restaurant.*

ii. (To refuse, reject an offer, invitation, application, request)

Examples:

- *Reluctantly, the university had to **turn down** his application.*
- *We've asked them round quite a few times, but they've always **turned** us **down**.*
- A: *If I promise to have the house done up, will you marry me?*
  B: *Look, I'm not **turning** you **down**, but give me time to come round to the idea.*

Note that Downturn is the opposite of **Upturn** (see Page 15, above), i.e. a negative change in the economy, trade etc,

e.g. *His speech about the economy taking a **downturn** came over quite clearly to the bankers at the conference.*

To afford (To have enough money to buy something/time to do something)

Examples:

- *On my salary, I don't think I will be able to **afford** such a posh car.*
- *There's no point (in) (my) having guitar lessons; I can't **afford*** the time.*

* If we mean money, it is not necessary to mention the word **money** but if we mean **time**, we must state it,

e.g. *I can't **afford** to go to the cinema* = money;
*I can't **afford the time** to go to the cinema* = time.

We can also use To afford to mean it wouldn't be advisable/sensible/it would be stupid to do something, otherwise you may suffer;

e.g. 1. *You can't **afford** to turn down an offer like that.*
2. *I'm not very keen on mobile telephones but, in my business, I can't **afford** not to have one.*

Handy

i.   (Useful, convenient)

Examples:
- *You must be really looking forward to moving; it'll be so **handy** living near the station.*
- *You may as well take an umbrella with you; you never know when it'll come in* **handy**.*
- *When your sister goes over to Japan, can you ask her to bring back one of those **handy** personal computers?*
- A: *There's a very affordable French restaurant around the corner.*
  B: *Oh, that's **handy** to know!*

* i.e. *when you're going to need it.*

ii.   (Nearby, with me/you etc.)

Example:
- *I don't appear to have his number **handy**. I'll have to get back to you with it this afternoon.*

Note that when **Handy** comes *after* the noun, it means **nearby**. Compare *Have you got a **handy** dictionary?* (i.e. useful) with *Have you got a dictionary **handy**?* (i.e. nearby).

To own up (To confess, admit guilt/ignorance, responsibility or incapability)

Examples:
- *The Government will never **own up** to being responsible for the downturn in the economy.*
- *When the young boy comes round after his operation, the police are going to try to persuade him to **own up** to the robbery.*
- *There's no point (in) trying to hide it; you might as well **own up** to the fact that you've no idea what you're doing.*

To go on

i.   (To continue, go ahead, last)

Examples:
- *I'm just going to turn down the television; please **go on** (with what you were saying).*
- *We can't **go on** like this! I can barely* handle it.*
- *This programme is very handy. It tells you exactly how long the show **goes on** for.*

ii. (To happen)

Examples:
- Unfortunately, he was reluctant to tell us what
   was **going on**/had **gone on**.
- It was a turn-up for the books. I didn't know there
   was so much **going on*** in this little town.

Note that this meaning of **To go on** is not generally used in the future. For example, one would **not** say What do you think will go on?

* i.e. there were so many things to do, a lot of entertainment.

iii. (To keep talking about something, complaining, or asking someone to do something)

Examples:
- I wish you'd stop **going on** about it;
   I've already apologised twenty times for turning up late!
- I'm sorry to **go on** at you, but could you please turn your stereo down?
- I'm going to **go on** at the Directors until they
   come round to my way of thinking.

iv. (To rely on as proof, to judge a situation after having seen or heard something relating to it)

Examples:
- As no one had owned up, the police had nothing more
   to go on than a blood-stained handkerchief.
- We really need something more concrete to **go on**
   before we can go on* with our enquiries
- I'm only **going on** what I've seen/heard but I have a strong
   feeling that she is going to turn down his marriage proposal.

* Note that it is not considered to be good style to repeat a word in a sentence. It is done here merely to show the different meanings of **To go on**.

v. (To go to another place after the one in question, to proceed to the next level or stage)

Examples:
- A: *What are you doing on your day off?*
  B: *Well, I'm going round to my mother's in the morning and then I'll probably **go on** to Sue's in the afternoon.*
- Wife to husband:
  W: *Come on, own up! What did you really do after the meeting?*
  H: *I told you; we **went on** to a Chinese restaurant.*
- *It was a turn-up for the books that he passed his advanced exams. We didn't think he was ready to **go on** to this level.*

*"I'm sorry to **go on** at you, but could you please turn your stereo down?"*
(see Page 18)

TELEPHONE CONVERSATION BETWEEN TWO FRIENDS:

JANE: *Hi Anne, it's Jane.*

ANNE: *Hello, it's been ages since I last heard from you. How are you?*

JANE: *Not too well, actually. I've had the flu for about a month. I take after my mum;
she's always ill.*

ANNE: *Hadn't you better call the doctor?*

JANE: *I'm rather reluctant to do that, and anyway there's no point. He can't help me.*

ANNE: *Yes, but you may as well see him. You could go on your day off.*

JANE: *I suppose so. I don't think I could cope with another month like the last one. I think you
are much better at handling illness than I am... Anyway, what's been going on in your life?*

ANNE: *I've just found a new flat. Actually, it's in a very posh street.*

JANE: *Show off! I bet it's lovely.*

ANNE: *Well, you know how choosy I am and I'm much better off than I was a few years
ago so I can afford to live in such an area. You'll have to come round when I've
got the place done up.*

JANE: *I'd love to. Incidentally, did your cat turn up? I asked round everyone at work but
no-one had seen it.*

ANNE: *Oh yes. He soon came back. He missed being made a fuss of and was fed up having to
survive on stale food.*

JANE: *What a turn up for the books! I thought he was gone forever...... I'm just going to
turn down the television. Hold on a second!*

ANNE: *OK.*

JANE: *Did you know, Manuel's parents are coming over from Spain next month? I'm quite
looking forward to it. I'd like to ask you over; they'd love to meet you. It will be very handy
having his mum here. She's a wonderful cook.*

ANNE: *Great! Unfortunately if it's next month, I'll have to turn you down. I'm going off to
France for a few weeks. Peter has a flat in the South and I thought instead of increasing
my overdraft by going to the Caribbean, I might as well go to France again, even though
I've been there quite a bit this year.*

JANE: *You lucky thing!..... I've just remembered; I still haven't got my* own back on *you for* going on *to my Mum about how I've* gone off *her cooking. You shouldn't have told her.*

ANNE: *Oh stop* making a fuss! *She asked me why you always* go on *to a Chinese restaurant directly after eating her dinner. I thought* what's the point in *lying? I'm sorry if I* came over as *being rather rude.*

JANE: *Don't worry. I was going to* own up to *her anyway. Would you like to* come over *tomorrow night, or are you busy?*

ANNE: *I have a few letters which must* go off *by Friday but I'd love to see you. What time shall I* turn up?

JANE: *Well, if you've got nothing better to do, you* may as well come over *to my place for dinner at about seven.*

ANNE: *Lovely. See you tomorrow at seven.*

DIRECTORS' MEETING

1st DIR: *Before we discuss the fall in this year's* turnover, *there are a couple of points I'd like to* go over. *Firstly, I must thank John for fixing the computer system when it suddenly* went off *last week. His in-depth knowledge of computers has really* come in handy. *However, we* can't afford *to let this happen again.*

2nd DIR: *I didn't* hear about *this. What's been* going on?

1st DIR: *We can't* afford the time *to go into details now, but I think some of the staff were all having an* off-day *at the same time and all I'm saying is that we can't* go on *like this.*

3rd DIR: *I think we'd be* better off *without a few of them. I know it's not always good policy to increase the* turnover *of staff, but if we want to reverse the* downturn *in trade we've been experiencing, we have to improve the quality of our staff.*

2nd DIR: *I wish somebody would tell me what all the* fuss *is about.*

3rd DIR: *Well, if you had* turned up *to our last three meetings, you'd have been aware of the* stalemate *we've reached.*

2nd DIR: *What on earth has* come over *you?*

1st DIR: *Now calm down!..... Wait a minute. I can hear the fire alarm* going off. *We'*d better go over *to the other office.*

CHILD: *Mum, have you heard about John?*

MOTHER: *No, what happened to him?*

CHILD: *Well, he was going off to night school when he saw a firework lying in the road. Not thinking that it was alive, he trod on it and the thing went off and burnt his leg. He was taken to hospital where they told him it might be quite a while before he can walk properly again.*

MOTHER: *You see, I've been telling you for ages how dangerous fireworks are. Have you come round to my way of thinking now?*

CHILD: *Not really, it was his fault for treading on the firework....... Oh yes, Mum?*

MOTHER: *What, my dear?*

CHILD: *That cheese you gave me for lunch yesterday had gone off.*

MOTHER: *Really?*

CHILD: *Either that or the bread was stale.*

MOTHER: *Impossible! You're just too fussy.......Oh, by the way: have you seen the handy camera your dad has just bought?*

CHILD: *Wow! He must have quite a number of them by now.*

MOTHER: *At least 5.*

CHILD: *Can I go out and play football with Peter now?*

MOTHER: *Only if you do your shoelaces up.*

CHILD: *OK. Bye.*

Chapter One: **Exercise**

CHOOSE THE CORRECT WORD FROM THOSE IN BLUE
Answers on page 204.

TWO BUSINESS ASSOCIATES MEET IN THE PUB AFTER WORK:

STEPHEN: *Hello Trevor, I haven't seen you for [1](long time/few/ages/year).*

TREVOR: *Yes, it must be quite a [2](number/often/few/while). I heard [3](about/of/from/with) your promotion. Were you expecting it or was it a [4](put/turn/keep/do) up for the [5](road/day/books/ time)?*

STEPHEN: *I must [6](own/take/speak/break) up, I was quite shocked. I had applied for a promotion last year but I was [7](turned/had/brought/put) down. I didn't think there was any [8](reason/point/ideas/ excuse) in applying again this year; I'd be [9](well/worse/good/better) off getting a job elsewhere. However, I [10](arrived/ran/turned/left) up to work last Tuesday and found a memo from the boss asking me to see him as soon as possible. I was a bit [11](unpleasant/pleased/happy/reluctant) to go to his office because I thought he was going to make a [12](complain/fussy/noise/fuss) about some work which I had recently done for him. However, he greeted me with the words, 'Well done, Stephen, your sales have helped us double last year's [13](turnover/expenses/tax/loss), and we would like to reward you with a promotion.*

TREVOR: *You must have been delighted.*

STEPHEN: *Well, I wasn't quite sure of its significance. He told me I'd have to move to our City office, but actually this is quite [14](boring/useless/handy/particular) for me because it's a direct line from where I live.*

TREVOR: *And you must be a lot [15](richer/better/poorer/well) off financially.*

STEPHEN: *Yes, I must say, it has helped me clear my [16](overdrawn/repayment/money/overdraft), and I've treated myself to a [17](posh/old/slow/renovated) car. How are things with you?*

TREVOR: *Not too bad. We're in the middle of [18](making /doing/do/done) up our house at the moment. We thought we [19](could/might/can/ should) as well, considering it hadn't been touched for fifteen years.*

STEPHEN: *I [20](bet/believe/wish/think) you're having fun!*

TREVOR: Well, actually it's not so easy. My wife is really ²¹(pretty/bossy/fussy/clever) and always expects me to ²²(come/be/turn/take) round to her way of thinking, but I keep telling her we can't ²³(want/sell/ afford/spend) half the things she wants, and one minute she chooses a colour for a room and the next minute she's ²⁴(taken/been/done/gone) off it.

STEPHEN: I know the feeling. I can't ²⁵(deal/cope/help/handle) my wife at all when it comes to shopping. She always ²⁶(speaks/goes/ plays/tries) on at me about my taste and then she buys the thing I chose in the first place.

TREVOR: Anyway, at the end of all this we'll be in the mood for our holiday. We're ²⁷(telling/walking/going/passing) off to the South of Spain for three weeks.

STEPHEN: That'll be nice.

TREVOR: Well, we've had a villa there for quite a few years. It has ²⁸(come/been/used/taken) in very ²⁹(convenient/handy/useless/good) during the summer holidays. I really look forward to ³⁰(go/going/coming/come). I love the way the Spanish ³¹(break/do/like/make) a fuss of my kids. They all ³²(come/go/move/ask) over as such warm friendly people.

STEPHEN: Yes it's true. The only problem for me is that I can't ³³(cope/handle/bear/endure) with the heat. Last time I went to Spain, it was so hot that I fainted. It took me quite a ³⁴(few/number/bit/little) of time to come round. My wife was quite anxious. She said a bomb could have ³⁵(gone/taken/exploded/broken) off, and I wouldn't have come ³⁶(up/down/free/to).

TREVOR: Really?........ Well, I've told Jim that I'd be ³⁷(coming/going/ running/flying) on to the club this afternoon, so I'd ³⁸(better/should/ really/ought) be on my way.

STEPHEN: OK. It was good to see you again.

24

The talks in Geneva between the Bosnian Serbs and Muslims have reached a [39]*(record/stalemate/draw/breakthrough) once again. The angry Muslim leader said that they had* [40]*(come/rent/gone/ask) over the same ground many times without success and that his people could not* [41]*(want/manage/succeed/afford) to give up more territory. The Serb leader, on the other hand, complained that the Muslims were just interested in* [42]*(making/getting/bringing/having) their own* [43]*(up/front/together/back) for the battles they had lost. The Muslim leader then accused the Serbs of* [44]*(showing/blowing/sharing/speaking) off their gains in the war. The UN mediator, who had* [45]*(brought/gone/come/been) over from Japan, said that he had never heard of any negotiations which had* [46]*(lasted/gone/made/continued) on for as long as these had, without a result.*

- - - - -

The Treasury has announced that there has been an [47]*(turn-up/change /worsening/upturn) in trade in the last six months and that the country could now* [48]*(able/afford/spend/pay) to borrow again. In addition, there were more people who could be considered to be* [49]*(well/worse/poorer/richer) off than at any other time since records began.*

- - - - -

Yesterday, a man was ordered to pay compensation for the nuisance caused by his car alarm repeatedly [50]*(coming/going/making/ringing) off in the middle of the night. One of his neighbours said, "I went to bed looking forward to my* [51]*(week/ holiday/year/day) off the next day but I was woken by this terrible piercing noise which* [52]*(went/gone/came/put) on for half the night. I wondered what was* [53]*(happening/trying/doing/going) on. I had a torch* [54]*(around/handy/convenient/ useful) which enabled me to see outside my house. There was a crowd of people gathered around this car shouting at one person in particular. The following morning the noise had stopped, but I was so tired I felt I* [55]*(should/could/might/would) as* [56]*(if/will /very/well) not have gone to bed.*

Chapter Two

Lesson One

All over

i.   (Throughout, in every part of)

Examples:
- *I know his book has sold* **all over** the world,*
  but he does go on about it!
- *I'm sorry, I've spilt my wine **all over** the floor.*
  Be careful not to tread in it.

Note the expression All over again which is an emphatic use of **again**, generally expressed in a *negative sense*,
e.g.   *I'm not going over it **all over again**; it's supposed to be my day off.*
* Note that To sell here has a passive meaning, i.e. *to be bought by the public.*

ii.   (Finished – often used for a difficult relationship or period of time coming to an end)

Examples:
- *Now that it is (**all**)* **over** between Jane and her boyfriend,*
  she should be able to afford the time to come round and see us.
- *The Prime Minister believes that once the War is (**all**)* **over**,*
  there will be an upturn in foreign trade.

* Note that the word **all** is not necessary for this meaning. It is used merely for emphasis.
Note that we often say that a person is all over the place (colloquial) when he/she is badly organised, either permanently or at a particular moment,
e.g.   1.   *I must own up; I'm **all over the place** this afternoon.*
        2.   *We had to turn her down; her CV was **all over the place.**

To work out

i.   (To calculate, think of a plan, devise)*

Examples:
- *You'd better **work out** exactly how much you are overdrawn by.*
- *The police will have to **work out** a way of acquiring more evidence;*
  so far, they haven't got much to go on.
- *Last year my colleagues and I **worked out** a new system of charging*
  the firm's clients, but the Board of Directors turned it down.

ii. (To succeed in understanding something/someone)*

Examples:
- *I can't **work out** what he's going on about; can you?*
- *We are trying to **work out** why the computer couldn't handle the data we fed into it.*
- *Even though I have known him for ages, I still can't **work** him **out**.*

* Note that American people often use To figure out instead of **To work out** for meanings i. and ii. only.

iii. (To be successful – often a relationship between people or a situation, business etc.)

Examples:
- *They went out together* for quite a while, but unfortunately it° didn't **work out**.*
- *You've been with our company for two months now and, reluctantly, we have to inform you that it° hasn't really **worked out**.*
- *The company's turnover is not looking very healthy at the moment, but I'm sure everything° will **work out** (fine).*

* Note that To go out with someone can mean to have a relationship with a person. It does not necessarily involve the physical act of *going out*.
° Note that for this meaning, only the impersonal subject can be used. **It** or **everything** refers to the relationship or situation. One could *not* therefore say *We/They are not working out*.

iv. (To end up costing, to amount to, – the final cost of something)

Examples:
- *I am not going over it all over again; I've already told you that it'll° **work out** at about £20,000.**
- *Go on, tell me the truth! How much do you think it'll° **work out** at?*
- *We thought that the holiday was going to be affordable but in the end, it° **worked out** (to be) very expensive.*

* This sentence means that after considering everything, this is about how much it will cost. Note for this use of **To work out**, we must add the preposition **at** if it is followed by a figure.
° The subject of this meaning of **work out** has to be **It**.

Up

i. (When a specific period of time finishes, often used in sports, competitions or exams with the word "time") **Colloquial**

Examples:
- On the tennis court:
  *Our time must be **up**. Anyway, I couldn't handle another game.*
- *Your trial period is **up** and we are sorry to say,
  it hasn't worked out (between us).*

Note that one would *not* use this to describe a holiday finishing. One could say instead,
Our two weeks' holiday is all over.

ii. (A problem, something wrong) **Colloquial**

Example:
- *I'll stop making a fuss when you tell me what's **up***.*

* i.e. *... what the matter is.*

iii. (To be awake and out of bed)

Examples:
- *I'm really looking forward to going to bed tonight;
  I've been **up** for more than twenty hours.*
- *Please don't go on all night about it; you're keeping me **up***.*
- *Don't wait **up** for me°. I've got a partners' meeting tonight
  which is likely to go on for ages.*

* i.e. *You're preventing me from sleeping/going to bed.*
° i.e. *Don't wait for me to come home before you go to bed.*
Note also *To stay up* which means not to go to bed,
  e.g. *We might as well let the children **stay up** late tonight, as they don't have school in the morning.*

Up to

i. (To have the choice, responsibility to decide)

Examples:
- *Yes, you're quite right; it may not work out.
  It's entirely **up to** you whether we go on with the project.*
- *I don't think we have very much to go on but we shouldn't be so
  concerned, as it's not really **up to** us to make decisions on these matters.*

ii. (To do) **Colloquial**

Examples:
- *I haven't seen you for ages. What have you been **up to***?*
- *Last weekend we did up the kitchen. What did you get **up to**°?*
- *I can't work out exactly what's going on but I'm sure he's **up to** something†.*

* What have you been up to? is a very common way of greeting a friend (either face to face or on the telephone) whom you have not seen for at least a few weeks. It simply means, *Tell me what's been happening in your life since I saw you last.*
Note that up to would *not* be used in the answer.

| | e.g. | A: | *What have you been **up to**?* |

e.g.   A: *What have you been **up to**?*
          B: *Nothing much, same as usual.*

° To *get* up to is used when the time has definitely finished, e.g. *last weekend.*
† This use of Up to with something has a negative meaning, in that the person is probably doing or planning to do something he or she should not do.

iii. (To feel well enough, capable of doing something – i.e. *to be/feel up to* doing something)

Examples:
- *I'd really love to come over tonight but, to be honest, I'm not/I don't feel **up to** it*.*
- *I'll do the Proficiency Exam in the summer, providing I am/feel **up to** taking it.*

* Compare with *To feel like doing something* which is much more general and simply expresses a desire to do/not to do something,
    e.g.   *I don't **feel like** going round to David's this evening.*
To be/feel *up to* doing something, on the other hand, suggests that the speaker has not been well recently and is still recovering.

iv. (Until, not more than, a maximum of – usually followed by a number)

Examples:
- *Landlord to tenant:*
  *I don't wish to go on at you about it, but, as I have already said, you've only paid **up to** 18th April.*
- *We had to turn down their offer; they were only prepared to go **up to** £50,000.*
- *I've heard quite a bit about that car. Is it true that it can comfortably fit **up to** seven people?*

Breakthrough (A sudden development/a dramatic step forward – often in research or negotiations)

Examples:
- *Recent medical research had reached a stalemate but now, I'm happy to say, there has been a **breakthrough**.*
- *News headlines:*
  *Today the Prime Minister reluctantly announced that a major **breakthrough** in the talks with the other European heads of state had not taken place.*

Clumsy (Describes a person who is always breaking and dropping things or falling over, or a very unnatural, complicated or careless way of doing something)

Examples:
- *Don't ask him round again! The **clumsy** fool broke three of my best plates.*
- *He handled the situation in a **clumsy** way/**clumsily**.*

Bossy (Describes a person who is always telling other people what to do)

Examples:
- *I can't cope with sharing a flat with him any longer; he's far too **bossy**.*
- *Don't be so **bossy**! If you want the radio turned down, do it yourself!*

Note that the verbal construction is To boss someone around/about,
e.g. *Just because you are having an off-day, it doesn't mean you can **boss everyone around/about**.*

Appalling*/Dreadful° (Very bad, awful)

Examples:
- *I wouldn't have asked for the day off, if I had known the weather was going to be so **appalling**/**dreadful**.*
- *The company's turnover last year was absolutely **appalling**/**dreadful**.*
- *We turned her down for the job because she behaved so **appallingly**/**dreadfully** at the interview.*

* Note the verb To appal/to be appalled which means to horrify, disgust/to be horrified, to be disgusted, often by the way someone behaves.
e.g. 1. *I was **appalled** by the way she treads on everyone.*
2. *His manners **appal** me; he takes after his elder brother.*
° As with the words Terribly and Awfully the word Dreadfully can be used to mean **really**,
e.g. 1. *I was **dreadfully** sorry to hear about your uncle's death.*
2. *He waited up for me even though it was **dreadfully** late.*

I could do with (I need)

Examples:

- *I don't really feel up to going out;* **I could do with** *an early night.*
- *I know it'll work out more expensive, but* **we could do with** *a better accountant.*

Note that the past of **I could do with** is **I could** *have done* **with**, which really means **I needed**,

    e.g.   *We went over the figures together last night; actually,* **we could have done with** *your help.*

Also note that **I can/could do** *without* is the opposite of **I could do** *with*, i.e. *I don't need, I could survive without*,

    e.g.   *It's up to you, but I think you* **can/could do without** *a car in London.*

Can may only be used with **without**. Therefore one would *not* say *I can do with*.

Note that *I can/could do without* can also mean, **I wish I didn't have** or **I wish I hadn't had** (i.e. *I could have done without*),

    e.g.   1.   **I could do without** *this dreadful man bossing me about all day.*

            2.   **I could have done without** *your assistance; you're so clumsy!*

To push in (To go in front of someone in a queue or waiting list without permission)

Examples:

- *Sorry to be bossy, but would you mind not* **pushing in**? *I've been waiting in this queue for ages.*
- A: *How did you manage to get treated by the doctor before anyone else?*
- B: *Well, I must own up; I did a bit of* **pushing in**.

To go down well (To be welcomed, well received, accepted – usually a decision, piece of news, a performer or a person who is introduced to others for the first time)

Examples:

- *The company's decision to ban smoking in the office was a turn up for the books and didn't* **go down well** *with most of the employees.*
- *I'm surprised to hear that such a typical English actor* **went down so well** *all over France.*
- *She married a well-off lawyer, didn't she? That/He must have* **gone down well** *with her parents!*

Note that one can use this expression in a question *without* the word **well**,

    e.g.   *How do you think it'll* **go down with** *your clients?*

To go/come down with (To catch an illness – e.g. *the* flu, *a* cold)

Examples:
- A: *Why has he got the day off?*
  B: *I think he has* **gone down with** *the* flu / a cold.
- *I don't feel up to going to the cinema.*
  I'm **coming down with** *something*.*

* Note that this expression is often used with **something**, suggesting that the person is becoming ill but he/she does not know exactly what it is. It is not used for anything serious.

To go down as (To be remembered by everyone in a certain way)

Examples:
- *Last year will** **go down as** *one of the most appalling in the company's history.*
- *This treaty will** **go down** *(in history) as being the first major breakthrough in peace negotiations between the super powers.*

* This expression is usually used in the future tense and is often followed by a superlative.

*"She married a well-off lawyer, didn't she? That must have **gone down well** with her parents!"*

(see Page 31)

Lesson Two

To catch up

i. (To reach the same level, position, place as another person/other people)

Examples:
- We'll **catch** you **up**/**catch up** with you later in the pub; at the moment, we're trying to work out what has been going on in the office.
- On the motorway:
  I'll never be able to **catch** them **up**/**catch up** with them; my car will only do up to 100kmph.
- Even if you take just one day off, you'll still find it difficult to **catch** the rest of the class **up**/**catch up** with the rest of the class.

ii. (To do/find out something – generally work or news – which one has not been able to do because of one's recent absence or lack of time)

Examples:
- I could have done without that meeting yesterday. It went on all day, and now I'm finding it difficult to **catch up** on/with all my work.
- What have you been up to? I'm dying to **catch up** on/with the news I've missed whilst I've been away.

To catch on

i. (To become fashionable, popular)

Examples:
- I don't think that those boots will **catch on** in London; they're too clumsy*.
- Even though he went down well in Italy, his music didn't really **catch on** in Germany.

* i.e. They have no elegance or style.

ii. (To be able to understand an explanation, situation or how to do something)

Examples:
- *We could do with an accountant like that. Did you see how quick* he was in **catching on** to what we were going on about?*
- *I don't think he realizes what his partners are up to but then he has always been rather slow* to **catch on** to what is going on.*
- *Everyone could see she was reluctant to talk about it, but your brother didn't **catch on** at all.*

* Note that this form of **To catch on** is often preceded by the words **quick** or **slow**.

Out of the blue (Suddenly, unexpectedly, for no obvious reason)

Examples:
- *We were just speaking about Mrs Smith when, **out of the blue**, she turned up at the front door.*
- A: *Did her husband know what she was up to?*
  B: *No, it came totally **out of the blue**.*

For the time being (For the moment)

Examples:
- *We'll probably catch up with the rest of the family in New York next year but, **for the time being**, we might as well stay in London.*
- A: *Where do you want me to put this dreadful painting of yours?*
  B: *Oh, leave it where it is **for the time being**, thank you.*

Note that this expression is used for a temporary situation; i.e. one which is likely to change soon.

To be/get stuck (To be unable to move or progress)

Examples:
- *I could do without **being stuck** in this queue. I've got so many things to catch up on back at the office.*
- Boss to secretary:
  *Would you mind handling this matter for the time being? If you **get stuck**, we'll go over it together next week.*

When one wants to express the idea of to fail or to run into serious problems, one can also use To come unstuck,

e.g.   1.   *If you don't learn to cope with your problems at an early age, you may **come unstuck** later on in life.*
       2.   *The Minister's decision to close down some of the coal mines did not go down well with the majority of politicians. The Government nearly **came unstuck** over the issue.*
(The word **over** in this example means in relation to.)

34

Also note the expression To be stuck for words, which means to be unable to give an answer or express oneself properly, often because of guilt, embarrassment or surprise,

e.g. 1. *He asked her what she had been up to but she was **stuck for words**.*
2. *I wonder what's up; it's not like him to be **stuck for words**.*

To stick to (To keep to, not to change or go away from a system, subject, advice etc.)

Examples:
- *I think we'd be better off **sticking to** just one method of teaching.*
- *Policeman to witness:*
  *If you had **stuck to** the truth, the trial wouldn't have gone on for so long.*
- *Don't worry, you'll catch on eventually,*
  *if you **stick to** what we've told you.*

Note the idiom To stick together which describes people who do not mix outside their circle,

e.g. *It didn't go down well, when I said to Luigi that Italians in London tend to **stick together**.*

Stuck-up (Snobbish – used to describe a person or attitude) **Colloquial**

Examples:
- *Not only is she bossy but she's also **stuck-up**;*
  she won't even talk to the cleaning lady.
- *I can't handle his **stuck-up** attitude towards the*
  other people in this firm.

To look into (To investigate a crime, problem etc.)

Examples:
- *As no one has owned up to the crime,*
  *we should let the police **look into** it.*
- *The Managing Director seems to be stuck for words, but his*
  *colleagues have promised they will **look into** the problem.*

Awkward

i. (Difficult, fussy)

Examples:
- *The final decision is up to you*
  *but it is a very **awkward** one to have to make.*
- *Please don't be **awkward**.*
  Just eat what you are given and stop making a fuss!

ii. (Embarrassed, embarrassing – an uncomfortable situation)

Examples:
- *I felt* slightly **awkward** when I realised that I was the only one who hadn't properly caught on to what was being said.*
- *It's so **awkward**° when you have to tell someone out of the blue that they are going to lose their job.*

* Note that one *cannot* say **I am awkward** to mean *I'm embarrassed,* because it means *I'm a difficult person.* One would therefore have to say **I** *feel* awkward (i.e. *I'm embarrassed*).
° **Awkward** in this example could *also* mean difficult (See **i.** above).

Apparently (It is said that, so I have heard/read)

Examples:
- ***Apparently**, they have the lowest turnover of all the major public companies.*
- A: *Is it true he owns three Porsches and a posh house in the South of France?*

  B: ***Apparently**!*

Apparently is used when the speaker is not completely sure of something. He is only saying what he has heard from other sources.
Be careful not to confuse **Apparently** with To be apparent which means obvious, clear,
e.g.   1.   *It is quite **apparent** that he feels awkward in strange company.*
         2.   *Everyone says he is a bit stuck-up, but it isn't **apparent** to me.*

To answer for

i. (To answer on behalf of someone)

Example:
- *I can't **answer** for my partners but I think the idea will catch on very quickly.*

ii. (To be held responsible/accountable for something going wrong)

Examples:
- *The public believe that the Government have got a lot* to **answer for** over the recent food shortages, and that the matter should be looked into immediately.*
- *I'm glad to see that the Directors have owned up to getting the company into this mess, but I still feel they've got a lot* more to **answer for**.*

* This meaning of **To answer for** is often used with **a lot to** and it suggests that the responsible person/people should explain why they have behaved so badly, been so unsuccessful or acted in such a negative way.

Hint/to hint

i.   (A piece of advice on how to do something, a tip)

Examples:
- *I've no idea what I'm doing; I could do with a few handy **hints**.*
- *I might as well ask Maria for some **hints** on Spanish cooking.*

ii.   (An indirect suggestion, to indicate something to someone in an indirect way, often because it would be considered rude or embarrassing to tell them more directly)

Examples:
- *He's a bit slow to catch on so we'd better drop* him a few, more obvious **hints**.°*
- *I can take* a **hint**! What you are really saying is that you don't want me to come round any more.*
- *The boss's secretary keeps **hinting** that she wants a new word processor, but he thinks she should stick to the old one.*
- *I don't know what he's going on about, but Anna seems to think that he's **hinting** at the possibility of new premises†.*

* Note that it is very common to use the verbs **To drop** and **To take** with Hint.
To drop someone a hint simply means to *give* someone a hint, whilst
To take a hint means to realise that someone is trying to tell you something negative in an indirect way.
° i.e. *We've already made some indirect suggestions but they weren't obvious enough. Therefore, we'd better make our hints a little more direct.*
† i.e. a new office.

*"The boss's secretary keeps **hinting** that she wants a new word processor, but he thinks she should stick to the old one."*

L e s s o n   T h r e e

To get (To understand a situation, explanation or joke) **Colloquial**

Examples:
- *I just don't **get** it! Why does he have to be so awkward all the time?*
- *It is quite apparent that he didn't **get** the point of what you were saying.*

Note the expression Don't get me wrong which means *Don't misunderstand me but...,*
    e.g.   ***Don't get me wrong**, but I think we could do without your brother running this business.*

To get to

i.   (To finish in a certain place, to arrive at)
Examples:
- *I'm stuck; can someone please tell me where* we **got to** last lesson?"*
- *Where* on earth did you **get to** last night?°*
  I knew you were up to something.

* This meaning of **To get to** is generally used with **where**.
° This suggests that the speaker was with the other person when he disappeared.

ii.   (To reach)

Examples:
- *Can you help me do up my dress? I can't **get to** the zip.*
- *Parents who allow their children to play with matches have got a lot to answer for; they should be kept where children can't **get to** them.*

iii.   (To annoy, irritate, move someone (emotionally) – usually after a period of time) **Colloquial**

Examples:
- *Her stuck-up attitude is beginning to **get to** me.*
- *A: What's up?*
  *B: Oh nothing really. It's just that the smoke in this pub is **getting to** me.*
- *His sad story really **got to** me... but I'm still a bit reluctant to help him.*

To sue (To bring a legal action against someone)

Examples:
- *If the company gets **sued** for non-payment of its debts, it won't go down well with the shareholders.*
- *I feel reluctant to **sue** them because even if we win, they can't afford to pay us.*

Note that for criminal cases the words To prosecute, prosecution are used,
> e.g. *At the moment, the police do not really have enough to go on to **prosecute** (bring a **prosecution** against) him.*

To be bound to (Very likely, almost certain to happen)

Examples:
- *Don't worry, he's **bound to** turn up; he's always late.*
- *She was **bound to*** have an accident; she drives so dreadfully.*

Bound literally means (legally) tied to something (e.g. a contract, rules etc.),
> e.g. *There's no point (in) discussing the matter. We are **bound** by the terms of the contract and we're stuck!*

Care should be taken not to confuse **bound** *to* with bound *for* which usually refers to a person, vehicle, letter, etc. heading in a certain direction,
> e.g. *The train on platform 4 is **bound for** Edinburgh.*

* As **Bound to** is used in the past in this sentence, it means that it was obvious she was going to have an accident and she did actually have one. Therefore, when **Bound to** is used in the *past* it means that the action or event occurred.

Thick (Unintelligent, not clever) **Colloquial**

Example:
- *I own up, I am a bit slow to catch on at times but I'm not that* **thick**!*

Thick does not describe a particular action, but someone's general intelligence and ability to understand. So one would **not** say to someone who had just done something stupid, *That was a really thick thing to do.*

* See the note for **Posh** (Page 11).

To keep up

i. (To continue – usually a hobby or payments)
Examples:
- *She takes after her aunt. She starts so many hobbies but never **keeps** them **up**.*
- *I couldn't afford to **keep up** the payments and so, under the terms of the contract, I was bound to return the equipment.*

ii. (To maintain a certain quality, to make sure something does not get worse)

        Examples:
- *Your dreadful appearance* has not gone down well with our guests and has made it difficult for us to **keep up** the standard of this hotel.*
- *I can see you're having an off-day today. You could do with a strong drink to **keep** your spirits **up**°.*

* Note the expression To keep up appearances which means to pretend that one is still rich or in love by doing the same things and behaving in the same way as one has always done,

    e.g.
    1. *They used to be very well off but, out of the blue, their business came unstuck and now they only turn up at posh parties **to keep up appearances**.*
    2. *Even though their marriage hadn't worked out, they went on living together just **to keep up appearances** to the press.*

° i.e. *to stop you getting depressed.*

To keep up with (To maintain the same level, speed as someone else, not to fall behind)

        Examples:
- *I got most of what he was (going) on about but he talks so quickly, it's hardly possible to **keep up with** him.*
- *You must **keep up**-to-date* **with** your homework, otherwise you'll find it difficult to catch up later on.*

* If **To keep up with** is *not* followed by a person, we often add **to date** in order to make the sentence sound more complete.

Also note the difference between **To keep up with** and **To catch up with** (see Page 34) and also **To keep someone up** (see Page 28).

To fall/land on one's feet (To experience success, find luck, contentment and security after a period of uncertainty)

        Examples:
- *Things are bound to be difficult when you first arrive in a foreign country, but don't worry, I'm sure you'll soon **fall on your feet**.*
- *Just when he thought he had **landed on his feet**, he was sued for breach* of contract.*

* i.e. for breaking the terms of a contract

40

To bump into (To meet someone you know by chance – i.e. without a previous appointment)

Examples:
- *I **bumped into** your cousin this morning and he told me that he'd been up half the night trying to catch up on some work.*
- *I'd rather not go into that pub in case I **bump into** my ex-partner; it could be awkward.*

Note To bump into someone/something literally means to strike or hit. We often use it for a minor car accident.

e.g. *I'm afraid I **bumped into** your car as I was coming out of the drive. You're not going to sue me, are you?*

Nasty (Unpleasant, horrible)

Examples:
- *Apparently, there has been a very **nasty** accident near the centre of town.*
- *Why are you so **nasty** to your sister? She can't help being thick!**

Note that someone who has a nasty streak in them is a person who has a very unpleasant side to his or her character which may not often be seen,

e.g. *Don't get me wrong; I like the man but he's definitely got a **nasty streak** in him.*

* i.e. *It is not her fault that she is unintelligent; that's the way she is!*

To take on

i. (To give someone a job, to employ someone)

Examples:
- *Even though we are in the middle of a recession, we have to **take on** more staff to keep up with demand.*
- *We should drop him some hints that if he doesn't like the job, we can easily **take** someone else **on**.*

ii. (To challenge – usually something/someone stronger or bigger – often in sport or politics)

Examples:
- *The new leader of the Opposition seems to have gone down well with the general public, and experts now believe they are ready to **take on** the Government at the next election.*
- *When this nasty weather is over, I'll **take** you **on** at tennis.*

iii. (To accept responsibility, work)

Examples:
- I've ***taken on*** *far too much work this week; I just can't cope with it all.*
- *We've asked her to* ***take on*** *the task of handling all our foreign clients.*

To stand for

i. (To be an abbreviation of)

Example:
- *I know it sounds silly, but these abbreviations really get to me. Can you tell me what I.T.U.* ***stands for****?*

ii. (To be a symbol of, to be associated with, to represent)

Examples:
- Politician speaking to voters:
  It is quite apparent that no-one knows what the opposition party ***stands for****.*
- *I hate stuck-up, posh people and all they* ***stand for****.*

iii. (To tolerate, bear a type of behaviour, to allow to continue)

Examples:
- *You know what she's like; she won't* ***stand for*** *any of this appalling nonsense.*
- *I can't answer for her but I certainly wouldn't* ***stand for*** *that sort of treatment.*

This meaning of **To stand for** is generally used in the negative, after **won't** or **wouldn't** and *not* **can't**. It can also be used in a question,
> e.g. *Why do you* ***stand for*** *it?*

However, it is not used with a person, but only a person's behaviour and should therefore not be confused with I can't stand which means **I hate** or **I can't bear**,
> e.g. *I can't stand* *that nasty man.*

iv. (To be a candidate for an election)

Examples:
- *He has really landed on his feet. At one time he was a waiter and now he's* ***standing for*** *President.*
- *John has been hinting that he intends to* ***stand for*** *Parliament next year.*

LETTER FROM LISA TO PATRICIA:

Dear Pat,

I've been meaning to write to you for ages. What have you been up to? I bumped into Alice the other day and she told me that you've just been taken on by one of the biggest banks in the City. You really have landed on your feet! I also understand that you've been dropping John some hints that you don't want to go out with him any more, but he's been too thick to take them. I don't want to be rude, but is it because he's so stuck-up or is it due to his nastiness, making you feel awkward in front of his friends? Anyway, it'll surely go down well with your parents; you always told me how appallingly he behaved towards them.

I've been trying to keep up to date with all my work but, to be quite honest, the job is beginning to get to me. Apparently, according to my boss, the firm is being sued by four companies who are owed money. Don't get me wrong; I like the people and the money's good but I could do with a change of scene. And besides, I'm not really up to doing the work which I've been asked to take on. The company used to stand for efficiency and honesty but recently it hasn't been able to keep up its standards.

I don't know if I've told you before, but my dad's intending to stand for Mayor this year. Personally I think he should stick to what he's good at, that is, being bossy at his office. I can't answer for the rest of the family but I think he's bound to come unstuck. Nobody can work out why on earth he wants to do it.

Anyway, I'd love to see you soon so that we can catch up on each other's news and gossip.

I wish you weren't living so far away!

All my love,

Lisa XXX

TWO BUILDERS WORKING AT A HOUSE:

BILL: *What's up?*

FRED: Peter's just spilled paint *all over* the dining room floor. I don't know why the boss *took on* such a *clumsy* idiot; and on top of that, last week he didn't get to work until 11 o'clock because he said he was *coming down with something*.

BILL: Apparently, it's *all over* between him and his wife but they are still living together to *keep up appearances* to the rest of the family. I feel sorry for the man.

FRED: I don't! I think he's got a *nasty streak in him*, and we *could do without* his stupid comments as well.

BILL: It's going to be *awkward* for the boss to dismiss him just *out of the blue*. *For the time being* he'll have to let him carry on.

FRED: I don't think he'll *stand for* his *clumsiness* much longer.

BILL: I must admit, he's a bit slow to *catch on*. But if you *look into* all the things *going on* in his life, you'll understand why nothing's *worked out* for him.

NEWSREADER:

There has been a major *breakthrough* in peace negotiations between the Serbs and Croats. They have signed a new peace treaty which will *go down as* the first major agreement between the two peoples. A spokesman for the European Community said that it was hoped that both countries would feel legally *bound* by the document, and that this current mood for peace would be *kept up*.

- - - - -

Today a man by the name of John Smith was *prosecuted* under the Noise Protection Act for *keeping his neighbours up* during the night with his parties. Neighbour, Hazel Coombes, said "We knew he was *up to something* when we saw him *pushing in* the queue at the Off Licence with three boxes of lager. My young kids were *kept up* for several nights because of him and his mates and I think he's got a lot to *answer for*.

When Mr Smith was told that his fine and legal costs could *work out* to be over £1,000, he was "*stuck for words*."

Chapter Two: **Exercise**

CHOOSE THE CORRECT WORD FROM THOSE IN BLUE
Answers on page 204.

TWO FRIENDS MEET IN THE STREET:

ALISON: *Hi Tracy, I didn't expect to* [1]*(meet/bump/look/break) into you today; I thought you'd be* [2]*(stuck/left/sent/stay) in the office.*

TRACY: *I usually am but today I thought I* [3]*(would/could/should/might) do* [4]*(from/to/for/with) a break from my routine. It's a pity the weather is so* [5]*(wonderful/raining/appalling/unclear). I can't* [6]*(think/catch/work/put) out why people wish to spend their summers here. Anyway,* [7]*(what/how/why/where) have you been* [8]*(coming/up/doing/down) to?*

ALISON: *I've been asked to* [9]*(catch/put/bring/take) on the responsibility of our overseas market and have been designing some new shoes which I hope will go* [10]*(up/in/into/down)* [11]*(properly/well/good/enough) in Japan.* [12]*(Obvious/Probable/Apparently/Possibly), it's the sort of design which is likely to* [13]*(catch/take/get/break) on there. My boss keeps dropping me* [14]*(suggestions/tips/hints/carefully) that he wants me to work weekends to get the job finished, but I won't* [15]*(cope/stand/put/handle) for that. Don't* [16]*(get/make/take/misunderstand) me* [17]*(right/mistake/wrong/incorrect), I'm not lazy but I have principles I like to* [18]*(make/stuck/stick/belong) to; such as, weekends are not for working.*

TRACY: *I don't blame you. Did you know my brother is* [19]*(stood/sitting/putting/standing) for the local elections?*

ALISON :   *No I didn't.*

TRACY: *Well, it's quite* [20]*(apparent/sure/apparently/reluctant) that no-one else wanted to stand so he thought he might as well do it. He's* [21]*(must/apparent/obvious/bound) to win. He's got the right* [22]*(pure/bossy/silly/clear) nature to be a politician.*

ALISON :   *I always remember him as being rather* [23]*(clumsy/stupid/violent/unpleasant) with your mum's china ornaments but the sort of person who* [24]*(flies/takes/lands/hopes) on his* [25]*(foot/feet/head/leg.) I can't* [26]*(question/spoken/live/answer) for the other people in this town but I'll certainly vote for him.*

TRACY: Oh, that's nice of you. I think his clumsiness was due to the fact that he always felt ²⁷(handsome/awkward/clumsy/happy) in front of you after your relationship was ²⁸(all/seen/eventually/often) over. It's a shame it never ²⁹(happened/turn/made/worked) out between you.

ALISON: Yes, I suppose so but it's all such a long time ago now. I know it came ³⁰(out/in/over/from) ³¹(of/off/at/from) the blue for him when I finished it, but we'd got to a stage where the relationship needed a ³²(new/ stalemate/ breakthrough/coming) of some sort. In the end, we were just keeping ³³(up/to/with/at) ³⁴(love/appearances/jobs/together).

TRACY: I think he was ³⁵(sticking/helped/probably/stuck) ³⁶(for/with/by/to) words when it first happened and since then, he hasn't ³⁷(gone/felt/ wanted/bothered) up ³⁸(like/about/to/with) trying new relationships. For the ³⁹(time/moment/now/present) ⁴⁰(been/gone/being/now) he wants to be on his own and concentrate on ⁴¹(trying/catching/catch/bringing) up with all his work......
           Do you know, this weather has made me feel ⁴²(well/good/dreadful /wonderful). I'm sure I'm ⁴³(coming/catching/taking/feeling) down ⁴⁴(from/with/against/without) something.

ALISON: I think the weather forecasters have got a lot to ⁴⁵(blame/deal/do/answer) ⁴⁶(to/by/with/for). They assured us that the ⁴⁷(great/nasty/predictable/raining) weather of last month was all over. It's a pity we can't ⁴⁸(warn/catch/sue/kill) them for getting it wrong!

TRACY: Oh well, it was lovely to see you again. Look after yourself.

*"I don't think that those boots will **catch on** in London. They're too clumsy."*
(see Page 33)

Lesson One

To take advantage of (To use someone/something for one's benefit, to exploit)

Examples:
- *You shouldn't let your boss **take advantage of** you like that; I don't know why you stand for it.*
- *We have a wonderful library in this office; I can't work out why people don't **take** more **advantage of** it.*
- *You should **take advantage of** the fact that it's working out well at the moment. Who knows what will happen tomorrow?*

When **To take advantage of** is used with a person, it has a negative meaning. Someone is being used or exploited purely for the benefit of the person taking advantage. On the other hand, when used with a thing or situation, it usually has a positive meaning, i.e. to enjoy the benefit of something.

To follow up

i. (To look into something*, investigate)

Examples:
- *I can take a hint! If you don't trust me, why don't you **follow** it **up** yourself?*
- *It's probably nothing to worry about, but you may as well **follow** it **up** just in case.*

* See **To look into** (Page 35).

ii. (To take further action after having said or done other things)

Examples:
- *I suggest you ring them first and make a fuss, and if that has no effect, **follow** it **up** with a strong letter.*
- *After telling him that he had a lot to answer for, she **followed** it **up** with even more verbal abuse.*

Note the noun and adjective Follow-up which means a continuation or additional part of something, e.g. a meeting or document,

e.g. 1. *This meeting is meant to be a **follow-up** to the one we had last December.*
2. *There will be a **follow-up** instruction sheet which we would like you all to take advantage of.*

Unheard of (Unknown, non-existent)

Examples:
- *She went down well with British audiences,*
  *although she is quite **unheard of** in her own country.*
- *Having a cappuccino in the evening has caught on all over*
  England but it's virtually **unheard of** in Italy.*
- *It is **unheard of** for her to turn up on time.*

See **To hear of** (Page 2).
*Virtually means the same as almost.

When it comes to (When considering, if you want to talk about)

Examples:
- ***When it comes to** making a fuss,*
  there's no one like my mother in law.
- *Certainly John has a lot to answer for, but **when it comes to** Mary,*
  if you look into what's going on in her life,
  you'll understand why she can be nasty at times.

Note the expression When it comes down to it which means actually, after considering everything,
  e.g. 1. *I know he has a bit of a nasty streak in him but, **when it comes down to it**,*
           he's not such a bad bloke / guy.*
        2. *He wanted to start his own business but, **when it came down to it**,*
           he couldn't cope with the responsibility.
* Note that the word Bloke is the British slang for man and the word Guy has the same meaning and is also used in American English.
Compare with When it comes to the crunch which means when a vital decision has to be made or action has to be taken,
  e.g. *He is meaning to do all sorts of things but I bet, **when it comes to the crunch**,*
        he won't have the courage.

To turn out

i.   (To result in, to become – in the end)

Examples:
- *I thought that going into business with them would be*
  *wonderful but it **turned out** to be a dreadful idea.*
- *We all believed that this time she had landed on her feet.*
  *It's such a pity; nothing ever **turns out** right for her.*
- *We had intended to look into the matter, but as it **turned out**,*
  it wasn't necessary because they all owned up anyway.

One should take note of the colloquial expression Hasn't it turned out nice? This expression is referring to the weather and the speaker is merely saying that earlier the weather was unpleasant but now it has improved. It is in fact a rhetorical question, i.e. an answer is not expected.

ii. (To produce – usually mass production of goods)

Examples:
- *They are trying to get their own back on us by **turning out** chairs with a similar design to ours. They'll never catch on!*
- *Her publishing company **turns out** up to a thousand books a week.*

iii. (To come together in a large number for a particular purpose, an attendance)

Examples:
- *It was quite a turn-up for the books; the whole of the company **turned out** to meet the new Managing Director.*
- *The **turn-out*** for the last general election was appallingly low.*

* Note the noun Turn-out. It is generally used with an adjective such as high, low, good etc. This example means few people voted at the last General Election.

iv. (To throw something/someone out of a place, to expel)

Examples:
- *We were **turned out*** of the restaurant for making too much fuss.*
- *Don't you think the house could do with a good **turn-out**?°*

* Compare with *We were turned away from the restaurant* which means we were refused entry. Note also the more informal expression To kick out which is used in relation to people only.
° i.e. *Don't you think we need to throw away the things we no longer use/need?* Note that the noun **Turn-out** can only be used for this meaning and **iii.** above (the second example).

v. (To be well dressed)

Example:
- *Even though it is quite apparent that none of the directors keeps up with the latest fashions, they were all well*-**turned out** last night when they stood for re-election.*

* This expression is generally accompanied by **well**.

Frown, To frown (A facial expression showing confusion, unhappiness, to look serious, unhappy, confused – the opposite of **to smile**)

Examples:
- *When I told her that I thought she was taking advantage of my mother, she gave me a wicked **frown**/she **frowned** wickedly at me.*
- *What's up? I've never seen anyone **frown** so much.*

Note that To frown upon means to disapprove of,

> e.g. *You can offer him a cigarette, but he's bound to say no; smoking is **frowned upon** in this office.*

This example means that although it is not illegal to smoke, it is presumed and expected that one will not do so. Therefore, **To frown upon** is slightly less emphatic than **To prohibit**. It is more often used in the passive voice.

Cosy (A small but warm and comfortable place, an intimate relationship, atmosphere)

> Examples:
> - *Now that they are retired, my grandparents will have more time to take advantage of their **cosy** cottage in the countryside.*
> - *Romantic relationships with clients are frowned upon in this firm. Things can get too **cosy**!**

* i.e. too familiar.

To give/hand in one's notice (To resign,* to give notice to one's employers that one is leaving the job)

> Examples:
> - *I cannot cope with this job any longer; I'm going to **give/hand in my notice** on Monday.*
> - *I understand that getting this new job would have been a real breakthrough for you, but you should have waited until after you knew for sure before **giving/handing in your notice**.*

Note also the expression To work out one's notice period which has nothing to do with the phrasal verb **To work out** (see Page 26). It literally means to work until the notice period has finished,

> e.g. *If you don't **work out your notice period**, it won't go down well with your next employer.*

* To resign is normally used for people in high positions such as directors, managers and union leaders etc.

To sack/to give someone the sack (To dismiss someone from a job)

> Examples:
> - *We only took him on last week, but he was so dreadful we had to **sack** him before his trial period was up.*
> - *She was given the **sack** because of her clumsiness.*

To bring up

i. (To raise and look after children while they are growing up)

Examples:
- *During the War we were **brought up** by our grandparents in a cosy country village.*
- *His parents **brought** him **up** to be polite. I can't work out why he's turned out to be so rude.*

Note the noun of **To bring up** is Upbringing,

e.g. *Even though he had a very poor **upbringing**, I'm glad to say he landed on his feet.*

ii. (To introduce a subject into a conversation, meeting etc. to mention something)

Examples:
- *He hinted that he would **bring** it **up** at the next meeting.*
- *I'd rather you didn't **bring up** my sacking in front of my parents again. I want to forget about it.*

*"His parents **brought** him **up** to be polite. I can't work out why he's turned out to be so rude."*

Lesson Two

To take for granted

i. (To regard something as natural without thinking about it, to presume)

Examples:
- Don't **take it for granted** that it will be easy to get a ticket; you'll have to queue for ages and you won't be able to push in.
- I **took it for granted** that I would be able to keep up the payments but now I'm overdrawn.
- Young people are bound to **take** their health for **granted** but they will come unstuck in later life if they keep up some of their nasty habits.

ii. (To take advantage of a person – often done unintentionally, to presume that someone will always be there to do things for you)

Examples:
- It is unheard of for my boss to say thank you for all the things I do for him; he simply **takes** me **for granted**.
- I've heard all about him; apparently, his wife cooks and cleans for him but he just **takes** her **for granted**.

See Page 48. **To take advantage of someone** is slightly more negative than **To take someone for granted** because in the former expression this way of behaving is usually done on purpose, whereas one might **take another person for granted** without even realising it.

*"I've heard all about him; apparently, his wife cooks and cleans for him but he just **takes** her **for granted**."*

To bother (To disturb/trouble someone, to make an effort to do something)

Examples:
- *Sorry **to bother** you, but I think your car alarm is going off.*
- Husband and wife:
  W: *We've asked them round quite a few times now, but they keep turning us down.*
  H: *I'm not **bothered**/It doesn't **bother** me whether they come over or not.*
- *If I had known you weren't going to turn up, I wouldn't have **bothered** going myself.*

* Note the expression *I/you/he etc. can't be bothered to do something/with someone* which means that the speaker is too lazy, too tired or is not in the mood to do something or it is too much of an effort to be with a particular person,

e.g.
1. *I **can't be bothered** to deal with it now. I promise I'll look into it first thing tomorrow morning.*
2. *Not only didn't she buy me a present but **she couldn't** even **be bothered** to come round to wish me happy birthday.*
3. *I **can't be bothered** with them any more; they're always making a fuss.*

To gather (To understand – *I've heard that*)

Examples:
- *I **gather** that there was a good turn-out at the council meeting last night.*
- A: *I bumped into your cousin last week.*
  B: *So I **gather**!*
- *From what I can **gather**, neither of them could be bothered to turn up.*

It is presumed that students already know the principal meaning of To gather, i.e. to assemble, come together,

e.g.
1. *I suggest you **gather** all your belongings before I turn out the rest of the house.*
2. *We might as well all **gather** in the reception area.*

To put off

i. (To postpone, delay something)

Examples:
- *The match has been **put off** until next Tuesday because of the appalling weather.*
- *When it comes to the crunch, he always **puts off** appointments with his dentist.*
- *Don't **put** me* **off** with your pathetic excuses! I'll go on at you until you agree to see me.*

* Note that it is *not* possible to **postpone** a person. However, **To put off** can be used in this way.

ii. (To distract, disturb someone's attention, concentration)

Examples:
- *I wish they'd turn their music down; it's **putting** me **off** my work.*
- *Please don't **put** me **off**; I'm trying to work out my tax bill for last year.*

iii. (To dissuade, discourage, to make someone reluctant/change their mind about doing something)

Examples:
- *The shop owner's bossy manner has **put** me **off** going back there.*
- *I was **put off** (the idea of) going to that hotel by my cousin. She said they made too much fuss of everyone.*

iv. (To spoil someone's pleasure in eating)

Examples:
- *Do you have to bring up the subject of your hospital operation now? You're **putting** me **off** my breakfast.**
- *The smell of stale eggs **put** me **off** my meal/food.**

Note that the adjective of **To put off** is Off-putting and could be used for all the above meanings except the first one (i.e. to postpone),

e.g.   1.   *The news he gave me was rather **off-putting**; I'll have to follow it up myself.*
       2.   *It's very **off-putting** eating at the same table as your brother; he has appalling manners.*

* This meaning of **To put off** is usually followed by a meal of the day (e.g. breakfast, lunch etc.) or the words *meal/food*.

Filthy (Very dirty)

Examples:
- *Your car's **filthy**. Don't you think it could do with a wash?*
- *His **filthy** jokes didn't go down well with the posh audiences he was performing in front of.**
- *When he told her what he had been up to, she gave him such a **filthy** look.**

* **Filthy** can be used in every sense of the word dirty, i.e. literally or to describe someone's use of language or a look of disgust.

Spotless (Very clean)

Examples:
- *I know we have made the floor filthy
  but I promise it will be **spotless** in an hour.*
- *I was brought up to keep my clothes **spotless**/**spotlessly** clean.*

Unlike **Filthy**, **Spotless** is generally only used to describe a place or object, rather than a person or use of language etc. However, it can be used to refer to someone's character or reputation to express honesty or respectability,
e.g. *This scandal will go down as a shameful error in an otherwise **spotless** political career.*

To call on/upon

i.   (To visit someone)

Examples:
- *When your sister comes over from France, please tell her **to call on** us.*
- *If I **call on** my doctor without an appointment,
  he'll simply put me off until the following week.*

Note the difference between **To call *on* someone** and To call someone which means to telephone a person.

ii.   (To request/urge a person/people to behave in a certain way or to take appropriate action)

Examples:
- *London Transport have **called upon** all staff and passengers
  to be extra vigilant during this period of terrorist activity.*
- *It's unheard of for the Managing Director **to call upon** all
  the staff to turn out to a union meeting.*

This meaning of **To call upon** is used on formal occasions only. The subject is usually someone in authority or a governing body.

To call off (To cancel something which has been arranged or planned)

Examples:
- *They were meant to have a shareholders' meeting tomorrow
  but, out of the blue, they **called** it **off**.*
- *They've decided **to call off** the Cup Final because of
  the nasty violence which occurred last year.*

Compare **To call off** with **To put off** (see Page 54).
Note that an object such as a train *cannot* be **called off**. **To call off** is generally used for meetings, strikes and other organised events.

It serves you right! *(You deserve the bad thing that has just happened to you!)*

Examples:

- *I warned you before that he would try to get his own back on you, and now look what's going on.* **It serves you right!**
- *I'm glad he was sacked; he couldn't be bothered to do any work.* **It serves him right!**

To break up

i. (To end a romantic relationship with someone*/the end of a relationship between/among people)

Examples:

- *At long last she has decided to* **break up** *with her stuck-up boyfriend.*
- *I wasn't particularly bothered when the Beatles* **broke up**.
- *When it came down to it, she couldn't handle the* **break-up*** *of her marriage.*

ii. (To finish, put an end to something* – as a transitive verb, usually a fight or disturbance – as an intransitive verb, a meeting)

Examples:

- *Local politicians are looking into the reasons why the police did not* **break up** *the violent demonstration.*
- *It didn't go down well with my wife when I told her the meeting wouldn't* **break up** *until 11pm.*

iii. (To finish a school term)*

Examples:

- *I am reluctant to go away until the kids* **break up** *(from school).*
- *I'm not looking forward to the children* **breaking up** *(from school); they'll be under my feet all day.*

iv. (To make a period of time seem more interesting or shorter by doing something different from the main activity)*

Examples:

- *I can't answer for my partners but I prefer to have my lunch out of the office because it* **breaks up** *the day.*
- *We could do with some light entertainment to* **break up** *the monotony of waiting for our flight.*

* Note that instead of **To break up**, To split up is often preferred in more informal conversation. However, unlike **Break-up**, it should *not* be used as a noun, (See Example i. above).

Lesson Three

Straightforward

    i.   (Easy, simple)

        Examples:
- *You're bound to find it; the route is very **straightforward**.*
- *A more **straightforward** approach to the problem is what we could really do with.*

Straightforward must not be confused with Straightaway which means immediately,
    e.g.   *You'd better leave **straightaway** if you don't want to bump into the boss.*

    ii.   (Honest, direct, frank)

        Examples:
- *You can't afford to put it off any longer. Just be **straightforward** with them and explain what's really going on.*
- *When it comes down to it, it pays* to be **straightforward** with your staff.*

* i.e. *You would be better off being straightforward...*

*"You're bound to find it; the route is very **straightforward**."*

Tricky (Difficult, complicated)

Examples:
- *I'm sure they'll come round to it in the end, but you must appreciate that it's a very **tricky** situation.*
- *The Minister for Transport was stuck for words when he was asked a few **tricky** questions.**

* Note that *a trick question* is one which is designed to deceive the respondent.

To cut out (To stop doing something – usually a bad habit, to stop working suddenly – e.g. a car)

Examples:
- *You'd be better off **cutting out** chocolate than potatoes if you want to lose weight.*
- *I was driving along the motorway when, out of the blue, the engine **cut out**.*
- ***Cut it out!*** Can't you see you're putting me off my work?*

Note the expression *To be cut out for/to do something* which means to be suited to a particular job or lifestyle,

e.g. 1. *Don't get me wrong, but I don't think you're **cut out to be** a lawyer.*
2. *I could do without this cold weather; I'm **cut out for** a life in the sun.*

* i.e. *Stop it!* This expression is probably more common in American English.

To cut down (To reduce)

Examples:
- *I've **cut down** from fifty cigarettes a day to just ten. I bet you couldn't do that!*
- *We'll have to cut out these expensive business lunches if we want to **cut down** on expenses.**

Note the expression *To cut someone down to size* which means to make a **show-off** feel small, humiliated.

e.g. 1. *He used to show off his wealth until she **cut him down to size** by telling everyone that he was overdrawn.*
2. *He was stuck for words; he didn't quite expect to be **cut down to size** in that way. It serves him right!*

* Note the difference between **To cut *out*** (See the above example) and **To cut *down***.

To put out

i. (To extinguish a fire, light, cigarette)

Examples:

- *Can you **put out** that cigarette? It's putting me off my dinner.*
- *The fire officer said that **putting out** the fire was not as straightforward as people thought.*

ii. (To cause someone inconvenience, to be upset, offended by someone's behaviour)

Examples:

- A: *The weather is dreadful tonight; would you like a lift home?*
  B: *Are you sure it's not **putting** you **out**?*
- *I've been going off him recently and I was very **put out** by the way he behaved yesterday.*

iii. (To make an effort to help someone, even though it causes inconvenience to the person helping)

Examples:

- A: *I gather that she put off going out with her friends in order to help her boss move house.*
  B: *That's interesting! She doesn't usually **put** herself* **out** for anyone.*
- *I know you usually play tennis on Sunday mornings but you should **put** yourself* **out** and go over to your grandmother's for a change; she needs fussing over.*

* This meaning of **To put out** is always used in the reflexive form and must involve some form of sacrifice.

iv. (To produce, publish – usually a formal statement or announcement)

Examples:

- *The Minister is about to **put out** a statement explaining why he hasn't followed the matter up.*
- *I took it for granted that we were going to **put out** another thousand brochures.*

Note the noun Output which means the quantity of production,
  e.g. *The **output** of the factory is not likely to increase for the time being.*

60

To nag (To annoy someone by continually telling or asking them to do something)

Examples:
- *My wife keeps **nagging** me to cut down on drinking.*
- *I'm sorry to **nag** you, but when will you come over to fix my television?*

To nag is very similar to **To go on at** (see Page 17).

To tell off (To punish someone verbally for doing something wrong, to scold)

Examples:
- *I don't know why you bother **telling** him **off**; he never listens.*
- *She's bound to **tell** you **off** if you turn up late to her dinner party.*
- A: *He was **told off** in front of his girlfriend for making his father's car filthy.*

  B: *That must have cut him down to size!*

To put up

i.   (To provide temporary accommodation for someone)

Examples:
- ***Putting** my parents **up** for Christmas turned out to be a lot less straightforward than we had imagined.*
- *I hope it's not putting you out, but would you mind **putting** me **up** for the night, as I've been turned out of my house?*

ii.   (To provide money to start a business or for a business deal)

Examples:
- *Despite the size of my overdraft, the bank has agreed to **put up** 70% of the capital.*
- *His father will give him a thousand pounds and his uncle's company will **put up** the rest. He has really landed on his feet!*

iii.   (To raise, increase the price, value of something)

Examples:
- *The only way to increase our turnover is by **putting up** our fees.*
- ***Putting up** the interest rates will go down as one of the main reasons why the Government failed to get re-elected.*
- *Doing up your kitchen and bathroom is bound to **put up** the value of your property.*

Note the expression To put up a fight which means to fail, lose or die after trying one's best against strong opposition,

e.g.   1.   *The visiting team **put up a courageous fight** but they were bound to lose with only five fit players.*

2.   *Let us remember those poor firemen who **put up such a brave fight**, attempting to put out this terrible fire.*

To put up with (To accept, tolerate a bad situation or person, to cope with*)

Examples:
- *I wish they would be quiet. I can't **put up with** that appalling noise any longer; it's putting me off my homework.*
- *I've gone off my neighbours but I suppose I'll have to **put up with** them.*

It is important not to confuse **To put up with someone** with To put someone up to something. The second expression means to make, persuade someone to do something wrong,

e.g.   1.   A: *I'll get my own back on you!*
           B: *It wasn't my idea; John **put me up to it**.*

2.   *Even though he owned up to the crime, the police believe someone else **put him up to it**.* (i.e. it wasn't his idea)

* See Page 12.

Rewarding (Worthwhile, satisfying)

Examples:
- *I thought the course was going to be a bore, but it turned out to be most **rewarding**.*
- *I realised that I had landed on my feet after finding this **rewarding** job.*

Note the difference between Reward and Award. A **reward** is something one is given in compensation or payment for a service performed. An **award**, on the other hand, is a prize one receives for winning a competition or being the best at something.

Also note that if a job is described as being Financially Rewarding, it means it is well-paid,

e.g.   *Even though her job is **financially rewarding**, she can't cope with it.*

62

A hold-up, to hold up

i.   (An armed robbery, to commit an armed robbery)

Examples:
- *The Christmas party at the bank was called off yesterday due to the **hold-up** that occurred earlier that morning.*
- *The two pensioners, who were **held up** in the high street, put up a brave fight.*

ii.   (A congestion, delay, to be delayed)

Examples:
- Radio announcement:
  *We advise drivers to avoid using the A6 because of a two-mile-long **hold-up** caused by roadworks.*
- *We are dreadfully sorry that we couldn't turn up earlier but we were **held up** in traffic for over an hour.*

MAGAZINE ARTICLE:

A Trip to London

I was very nearly put off the idea of visiting London by my sister who told me the streets were filthy and you could be held up by muggers, if you found yourself in the wrong part of town. However, I've had a rewarding experience here, having been put up by a friend in a cosy semi-detached house which he has kept spotlessly clean just for my benefit. I have taken advantage of his hospitality and he has put himself out to make me feel at home. I don't really want to bother him, but, as it turns out, he rather enjoys being a host and guide.

The only thing I found to be a bit tricky is driving on the left , but, when it comes down to it, it's worth getting used to – I just can't be bothered to take the tube. I do find some of the customs a bit strange too; for instance, it's quite unheard of in my country to see adults eating chocolate whilst walking down the street. I'd get severely told off if I did that back home.

Yesterday, we were thinking of calling on the Queen but, unfortunately, she wasn't in. I gather that she's trying to cut down on Royal visits, but there are some which she just can't call off. I must admit, I was a bit put out to be turned away from St Paul's Cathedral because I had no change for the entrance fee! I took free entrance to a church for granted. What on earth has come over these people?

The worst thing I've had to put up with is the unpredictable weather. Last Saturday a group of us gathered together under Big Ben. Our guide's first comment was "Hasn't it turned out nice?" and then, out of the blue, the rain came down. We all frowned in frustration but we knew it served us right... We had been warned: "Take an umbrella wherever you go!"

JULIE: *Have you heard about Steve?*

ANGELA: *No, what's up?*

JULIE: *He's* handed in his notice. *Actually he'd probably have been* sacked *anyway. Apparently, the other day the boss was very* straightforward with *him and told him that no-one was prepared to* put up with *his* nagging *any longer and he was* putting people off *their work. If you see him, don't* bring *it* up.

ANGELA: *No, of course not. Hasn't he just* broken up with *his wife?*

JULIE: *Yes, and he keeps trying to* put off *the divorce because he can't afford to pay for the* upbringing *of his two kids, and also he still loves his wife dearly. She claims she* went off *him when he started* taking her for granted.

ANGELA: *Is he going to have a big leaving party?*

JULIE: *Yes, next Friday. I hope there'll be a good* turn-out *for it.*

ANGELA: *Look at that* guy*! This is supposed to be the non-smoking part of the restaurant. If he doesn't* put his cigarette out, *he should be* turned out *for* putting people off *their dinners. It's a shame because I really enjoy coming here; it* breaks up *the day and they haven't* put up *the prices for over a year.*

JULIE: *Yes it is nice here, but I wonder what's* holding up *our chicken. The waitresses are well* turned out *here but they're a bit slow.*

ANGELA: *Do you want me to* follow it up *or do you think making a fuss is* frowned upon *in this restaurant?*

JULIE: *No, don't worry. Maybe the oven has* cut out *or the chef is* breaking up a fight *between two cooks.*

ANGELA: *I'm sure there's a more* straightforward *reason than that!*

Chapter Three: **Exercise**

CHOOSE THE CORRECT WORD FROM THOSE IN BLUE
Answers on page 204.

THOUGHTS OF A BORED HOUSEWIFE:

I know the house is 1(clean/healthy/filthy/dirt) but I really can't be 2(bother/bothered/worried/care) to do any cleaning today – I'll 3(do/put/take/have) it off until tomorrow. My husband keeps 4(nagging/making/bossing/saying) me to keep the place 5(spotless/dirty/filthy/wet) but he'll have to 6(cope/handle/put/catch) up with the dirt. I don't find being a housewife 7(boring/happy/friendly/rewarding). I'm not 8(put/cut/made/designed) out for it at all. In fact, if it were considered to be a real job, I'd 9(take/put/push/give) in my 10(books/job/notice/certificate); although thinking about it, I would have been 11(sacked/hired/employed/forgotten) ages ago. When it 12(breaks/comes/makes/plays) down to it, I'm bored. It is 13(heard/spoken/unknown/unheard) of for my husband to help me in the house. He just 14(takes/gives/has/brings) me for 15(ever/now/granted/accepted). When we got married, I thought he was going to be a modern, liberal-thinking man, but he has 16(comes/turned/went/put) out to be the same as all the others. He thinks it is my duty to 17(raise/kick/pull/bring) up the kids and doesn't see why he should 18(put/bring/take/make) himself out to take them to school and help them with their homework. For him, life is very 19(tricky/straightforward/difficult/sufficient). He works, comes home, has his dinner and goes to bed. There's no point in putting up a 20(game/brave/fight/dance). He'd only 21(whisper/cry/frown/pretend) and say:"Am I such a bad husband?"

In fact he isn't. I love him dearly and would never think of 22(breaking/split/bringing/staying) up with him. Also, I wouldn't want to 23(take/put/make/get) my daughters off marriage, but I'd certainly tell them not to let themselves be taken 24(careful/after/granted/advantage) of.

12 The Dell
ST ALBANS
Herts
1st March 2006

Manager
ABC Stores Ltd
High Street
PLAIDSTONE

Dear Sir,

Last week my kids 25(stayed/went/broke/broken) *up from school and I decided to take them to your Summer Sale to buy them some new clothes for our holiday. I* 26(gather/assume/presume/got) *that the store closes at 6.00pm and we arrived at ten to six, only to be turned* 27(up/out/back/away) *by the security guard for being too late. I was most* 28(work/put/turned/brought) *out because I had made a special journey. After much protesting, I was finally allowed in and quickly chose some clothes for my children. I made my way to the main pay desk, as did many of the other people who had* 29(picked/turned/come/gone) *up for your Summer Sale. There was a* 30(robbery/delay/hold-up/stick-up) *in my queue because the till had suddenly gone off. By the time they had got it working again, it was already five past six and, just when it was my turn to be served, we were all told that the sale had officially finished and no more discounts were to be given. I couldn't believe my ears! When I complained to the Floor Manager, she said it* 31(deserves/warned/held/served) *me right for leaving it so late. I* 32(shouted/spoke/told/said) *her off for being so rude, but she seemed to find it funny.*

I complained to your head office and I was told to 33(follow/look/investigate/continue) *it up with a letter which is why I have written to you today. In the past, I have* 34(brought/left/given/taken) *your good service for granted, but now it appears that politeness and good manners are* 35(discouraged/frowned/smiled/prohibited) *upon. I call* 36(upon/off/in/down) *you to* 37(pick/bring/have/get) *this matter up with your staff who were on duty last week. I must be* 38(directly/honestly/polite/straightforward) *with you and say that until I receive an apology and assurance that it will not happen again, I shall be taking my custom elsewhere.*

Yours faithfully,

MARY PHILLIPS

Chapter Four

Lesson One

To turn into (to change completely, transform)

Examples:
- *It may well* have started as a discussion but it soon* **turned into** *a fight; at least, that's how it came over to us.*
- *He is a very pleasant bloke socially but when he's at work, he* **turns into** *a monster.*
- *We could do with more space in this house. Maybe we should* **turn** *the garage* **into** *an extra bathroom.*

Note that **To turn into** can sometimes be used in a similar way to **To turn out to be** (see Page 49). The difference really is in emphasis. **To turn into** stresses a change, whilst **To turn out to be** is more concerned with what happens in the end.

Therefore, **To turn out to be** could *not* be used in the last two examples above, but where the stress could be either on the idea of a transformation (**To turn into**) or the final result (**To turn out to be**), both can be used,

e.g. *He was a nasty, bossy child but he* **turned into/turned out to be** *a charming young adult.*

* Note that It may well has nothing to do with It may as well (see Page 5). It may well is simply a more emphatic way of saying It may, i.e. possibly.

To do something in one go (To start and finish something without stopping)

Examples:
- *I thought he had cut out alcohol, but last night I saw him drink three vodkas* **in one go**.
- *This book has been frowned upon by critics, but I found it so exciting that I finished it* **in one go**.

If someone says It's your go whilst playing a game such as cards, chess etc., it means **It's your turn to play**,

e.g. *Go on!* **It's your go**.

To have a go

i.   (To try something to see if one is able to do it)

Examples:
- *My mum thinks I'm too clumsy to be a ballet dancer but I'm going to* **have a go** *(at it) anyway.*
- *I don't think we'll be able to push in but we may as well* **have a go**.

One could use To give it a go in the same sense,

e.g. *They don't think their relationship will work out but they're going to* **give it a go** *just to make sure.*

ii.   (To tell off*, criticise strongly) **Colloquial**

Examples:
- *She gave in her notice this morning, just because the boss **had a go** at her for being late.*
- Boss to two employees:
  __Having a go__ at each other in the reception area doesn't go down very well with our clients.

* See Page 59.

To go

i.   (To be left, to be remaining)

Examples:
- *He's only got two years **to go** before he retires; I'm sure he'll turn into a little boy again when he has all that time on his hands.**
- *There are only two weeks **to go** until Christmas, but I'm not really looking forward to it.*

* i.e. a lot of spare time.

ii.   (To match in colour, to be the right colour)

Examples:
- *I'm sorry to make a fuss, but that tie does not **go** with your jacket.*
- *Give me a straightforward answer! Do you think that my skirt and handbag **go** well together?*

One should be able to distinguish between **To go** (see examples above), To suit which means to look good,

    e.g.   *You could do with another haircut; that one doesn't really **suit** you,*

and To fit which means to be the right size,

    e.g.   *I've gone off colourful jackets and anyway, this one doesn't **fit** me.*

*"Give me a straightforward answer! Do you think that my skirt and handbag **go** well together?"*

69

To go/drive somebody round the bend/up the wall (to go or to make someone crazy/mad or angry)

Examples:

- *I've got so many dreadful things and people to put up with in the office that sometimes I feel like I'm **going round the bend**.*
- *Isn't that music from next door putting you off your work? It's **driving me round the bend/up the wall**!*

The difference between **To** *go* **round the bend** and **To** *drive* **somebody round the bend** is that the first is intransitive (i.e. there is no direct object) and the second is transitive (i.e. it has a direct object – *somebody*).

To trip up/over (To fall over/to hit something with one's foot, causing one to fall or almost fall)

Examples:

- *I can't believe how clumsy I was yesterday; firstly, I trod on someone's glasses and then I **tripped over** this bloke's briefcase.*
- A: *What on earth have you done to your arm?*
  B: *Oh, I **tripped up/over** yesterday on my way to the shops and no one put themselves out to give me a hand.*

Note that only **To trip** *over* can be used in the first example, i.e. one cannot use **To trip up** plus an object unless it is a person *tripping someone else up*, or when one falls as one goes up the stairs,

e.g.   1.   *The nasty pupil **tripped the teacher up** as he entered the classroom.*
       2.   *Someone's bound to **trip up** these stairs; they are so uneven.*

To Swap (To exchange)

Examples:

- *Even though I sometimes feel that I can't put up with my husband any longer, I wouldn't **swap** him with/for* anyone else.*
- *Can we **swap** calculators? I can't work out how to use this one.*

* The difference between **with** and **for** when used with **To swap** is that **with** relates to the owner of another object being swapped (in this example, another wife), whilst **for** relates to the other object itself (i.e. another husband).

To try on (To wear clothes for the first time – usually before buying them)

Examples:

- *Yesterday, in the local department store,*
  *I tripped over a coat hanger as I was **trying on** a jacket.*
- *I'm going to **try on** my new shirt to see*
  whether it goes with my trousers.

Note the colloquial expression To try it on with someone which has three meanings:
1. To try to trick someone.
2. To see how far one can go with someone before they react.
3. To show someone that one is interested in them sexually/To try and seduce someone,
   e.g. 1. *Don't even think of **trying it on** with me; I know exactly what you're up to!*
   2. Mother to father:
      *The children have been **trying it on** all day; they're driving me up the wall.*
   3. *John had a go at his neighbour for **trying it on** with his wife.*

To make out

i. (To try to understand a situation or a person, to work out*)

Examples:

- *I can't **make out** why he keeps putting off the wedding.*
- *Can you **make out** what on earth is going on?*

* See Page 26.

ii. (To identify with difficulty by sight or hearing)

Examples:

- A: *Can you see Peter, right at the*
  back of the queue trying to push in?
  B: *Oh yes, I can just about **make** him **out**.*
- *The telephone line was so appalling, I could barely**
  ***make out** a word he was saying.*

* Barely means the same as **Hardly**.

iii. (To claim, to pretend that, to give the impression that)

Examples:

- *He **makes out** that he is poor but actually he's quite well-off.*
- *She **made out** that she had never heard of our company.*
- *His mother **makes him out to be** a saint but,*
  when it comes down to it, everyone knows he's a dreadful person.

iv. (To write a cheque to someone, prepare a receipt, list etc.)

Examples:
- *Before this letter goes off, you'd better find out who we **make** the cheque **out** to.*
- *Sorry, but I'm not authorised to **make out** receipts. I hope it doesn't put you out at all.*

Upside down (Something is in the opposite position to what it should be, i.e. the top is at the bottom and vice versa)

Examples:
- *I can't make out a lot of modern art. For example, that picture looks **upside down** to me.*
- *After the bomb went off, I was shocked to see how many cars were turned **upside down**.*

Another way of saying **upside down** is the *wrong* way up, the opposite of which is obviously the *right* way up,
    e.g.   *They stuck the picture on the wall **upside down**. Can you please turn it **the right way up**?*
Also, Upside down can be used figuratively to mean disorder, mess and confusion.
    e.g.   *My life is totally **upside down** at the moment; I think I'm going round the bend.*

On the ball (To be up-to-date with modern developments, ahead of others, quick to catch on*, to know what is happening – especially in business)

Examples:
- *The last solicitor we had was a bit thick, but this one appears to be **on the ball**.*
- *I couldn't make out a word he was saying, but maybe it's because I'm not really **on the ball** today.*

* See Page 33, ii.

To make up

i. (To invent a story, to make a speech without referring to notes)

Examples:
- *Don't try it on with me! I know you're just **making it up**.*
- *I can't be bothered to prepare notes before giving a speech; I just **make it up** as I go along.**

* i.e. *as I'm speaking.*

ii. (To become friends again after an argument)

Examples:
- *Last night they were having a terrible go at each other, but I gather that they've **made up** this morning.*
- *I took it for granted that, after the last argument we had, we would **make up**, but it hasn't turned out like that at all.*

iii. (To form, consist of)

Examples:
- *Student fees **make up** most of our turnover.*
- *I haven't heard that much about it but, apparently, the committee is **made up** of doctors, engineers and builders.*

iv. (To compensate in time, money or by some positive action, to pay the balance)

Examples:
- *He has spent quite a bit of time away from his children lately but he promises to **make it up** to them/ **make up** for it next weekend.**
- *She says that nothing will **make up** for the way he has taken advantage of her over the last few years.*
- *The bank have said that if we can put up £600,000, they will **make up** the difference.°*

* Note the different constructions **To make it up** *to someone* but **To make up** *for something*.
° It is usually another person or organisation that **makes up the difference**.

To make up one's mind (To decide)

Examples:
- *I still haven't **made up my mind** whether or not I want to bring it up at the next meeting.*
- *I've **made up my mind*** to hand in my notice because I could do with a change of scene.*

* When we use **To make up one's mind** to do something, it suggests that we have been thinking of doing it for quite a while.

Lesson Two

To pick up

i.   (To collect someone, to raise from the ground)

Examples:
- *I'll be round to **pick** you **up** at 9 o'clock.*
- *Can you **pick up** my pencil before someone treads on it?*

ii.   (To understand and learn something by practice and experience rather than by study)

Examples:
- *When I was over in China last year,*
  *I managed to **pick up** a little Cantonese.*
- *She is very quick to **pick** things **up*** because she*
  takes after her mother, who was also really on the ball.

* This use of **To pick up** is very similar to **To catch on** (see Page 33). However, note that one cannot **catch** *things* **on** but only **catch on**.

iii.   (To acquire, obtain, purchase)

Examples:
- *I was under the impression that Japanese universities turned out*
  students with American accents, but you seem to have
  ***picked up** an English one.*
- *I don't know where you **picked up** that idea*
  but it won't go down well with the boss.
- *I gather that you **picked up** this wonderful old clock at an auction.**

* When meaning to purchase, **To pick up** usually indicates that the article was a bargain and/or perhaps very rare and old.

iv.   (To catch an illness)

Examples:
- *I don't know where I **picked up** this cold but it's lasting ages.*
- *I was put off the idea of travelling through jungles;*
  *my brother **picked up** malaria in that way.*

v. (To improve, get better)

Examples:
- *Business has been slow recently but it's bound to* **pick up** *in the new year.*
- *He is still seriously ill but he has* **picked up** *quite a bit in the last few days.*

Note that unlike meaning **iv**, this use of **To pick up** is intransitive i.e. one cannot say *I'm picking up my cold* but simply *I'm picking up.* This meaning of **To pick up** is generally used in relation to business or health.

vi. (To discuss something which has already been mentioned but in more detail)

Examples:
- *I wonder if I might** **pick up** *the point Arthur brought up just a few moments ago.*
- *I would just like to* **pick up** *on what I was going on about yesterday.*

Note the expression **To pick up where one leaves off** which means to begin again at the point where one finishes,

      e.g. *If someone can tell me where we got to last lesson, we can* **pick up where we left off**.

* **I wonder if I might** is an even more polite way of saying **Please may I**.

vii. (To arrest – usually for a minor offence)

Examples:
- *Quite a number of the people who turned up for the demonstration were later* **picked up** *by the police for being drunk and disorderly.*
- *Apparently, he has been* **picked up** *again for speeding.*

viii. (To notice, detect – often errors or something wrong)

Examples:
- *Perhaps you found one or two mistakes but there are bound to be others that you haven't* **picked up** *yet.*
- A: *I felt that she was dying to call off the wedding.*
- B: *Yes, I* **picked** *that* **up** *as well.*

ix. (To correct or criticize someone on matters of minor importance – to pick someone up on something)

Examples:
- *She's so fussy; she'll* **pick** *you* **up** *on every tiny detail.*
- *I could really do without him* **picking** *me* **up** *on everything I say.*

x. (To meet someone unknown with the aim of having a short sexual relationship with them) **Slang**

Example:
- *I'm not cut out for **picking up** women in discos; I'm too shy and I don't like them to think I'm trying it on (with them).*

xi. (To be responsible for paying a bill)

Examples:
- *Don't worry! You go on to the club and we'll **pick up** the bill.*
- *Landlord to tenant: You'd better ask the plumber to call on you as soon as possible but tell him that I'll **pick up** the bill.*

To pick up *cannot* be used in every sense of paying a bill. For example, one would not say *I cannot afford to pick up my telephone bills.* With **To pick up**, the emphasis is on the *responsibility* rather than the actual paying of the bill.

xii. (To find a station on the radio)

Example:
- *He says that he can **pick up** Russian radio on his small transistor but I think he is making it up.*

The other way round (The opposite to what has been said or thought – must involve two things or people)

Examples:
- *She makes out it's his fault, but everyone knows it's **the other way round**.*
- A: *John's bossy and Peter's clumsy; is that right?*
  B: *No, (it's) **the other way round**.*

Hectic (Very busy)

Examples:
- *I've had an extremely **hectic** day in the office today, so would you mind if I got back to you tomorrow?*
- *I'm not cut out for city life; it's far too **hectic** for me.*

Note that **Hectic** cannot be used for a person, i.e. one *cannot* say *I am hectic* but one can say *My life is hectic* or *Things are hectic.*

To get away with (To do something wrong and not be punished for it)

Examples:
- *He was picked up for speeding and careless driving but, somehow, he **got away with** it.*
- *She **gets away with** coming in late and taking long lunch breaks because she puts up the boss's mother whenever she comes over from Italy.*
- *Apparently, she's had cancer for years, but the hospital failed to pick it up. They shouldn't be allowed to **get away with** it.*

Note that it is very common to follow this expression with the word **murder**. To get away with murder literally means someone has murdered another person and has not been punished. However, it is usually used in a figurative sense, i.e. someone can do what they want without fear of punishment or discipline,

e.g.   *Her children are not brought up very well; in fact, she lets them **get away with murder**.*

To let (someone) off (Not to punish someone who has done something wrong)

Examples:
- *If the police had had something more to go on, the men wouldn't have been **let off** so easily.*
- *Why should we **let** him **off**? We all know he's up to something.*

When discussing a crime or other wrongful act, the difference between **To let someone off** and **To get away with something** is that the first expression relates to the person in authority, i.e. the person who is allowing the guilty party to go free, whilst the second one refers to the person who has done the wrongful act,

e.g.   Policeman to Boy:
       *I'll **let you off** today but if I catch you here another time, you won't **get away with it** again.*
       i.e. the policeman does the **letting off** and the boy **gets away with it**.

To go through/hit the roof (To get very angry, to lose one's temper)

Examples:
- *I nearly **went through the roof** when I discovered that they had made the cheque out to my ex-wife.*
- *Don't take it for granted that he's going to let you off. I think he'll **hit the roof** when he finds out what you've been up to.*

Note that To go through the roof can also be used to describe prices, interest rates etc. which have risen sharply,

e.g.   *Although business has picked up lately, it has meant that property prices have **gone through the roof** again.*

Also note that one *cannot* **hit the roof** *with* someone. In this instance one must use To lose one's temper.
Finally, one should note the expression To fly off the handle which is another less common way of saying **To lose one's temper**,

e.g.   *I'm sorry I **flew off the handle** (at you) yesterday but I was having such an off-day.*

To be off (Going) **Colloquial**

Examples:
- A: ***I'm off*** *now.*
  B: *Thanks for putting yourself out for me today.*
      I really appreciate it.
- Mother to daughter:
  I wondered where you got to last night... and where are you **off to** *now?*
- *I'm looking forward to my holidays.* ***I'm off*** *to* France on Monday.*

* See **To go off** (Page 4).

Dodgy (Not very good, not to be trusted, risky, doubtful) **Slang**

Examples:
- *I don't know if he's really nasty, but there's definitely something* **dodgy** *about him*
- *The weather's looking a bit* **dodgy** *today. We'll probably have to put the match off until next month.*
- *I shouldn't bother* taking me on if I were you; my tennis is very* **dodgy**.

Dodgy is a very popular word in British slang and is used and understood by all levels of society. It comes from the verb To dodge which means to avoid.
- e.g.   1.   *You'd be better off leaving early, if you want to* **dodge** *the traffic.*
-        2.   *The Managing Director of London Transport warned that, from now on, no one will be allowed to get away with fare-***dodging**.

* i.e. *It's not worth challenging me to a game.*

How come? (Why? why not?) **Slang**

Examples:
- ***How come*** *you didn't* turn up at the party?*
- A: *I couldn't make out a word he was saying.*
  B: ***How come?***

* Note that we do *not* invert the verb as we do with **Why?**
- e.g.   1.   *Why* **didn't you** *tell me?*
-        2.   *How come* **you didn't** *tell me?*

Neither do we use the auxiliary verb **do** in positive questions;
- e.g.   1.   *How come you always ignore me?* – **but**
-        2.   *Why* **do** *you always ignore me?*

To get over

i. (To recover from shock or illness)
Examples:
- There's nothing that can make up for the loss of her husband; she'll never **get over** his death.*
- I don't feel up to going out tonight; I'm still **getting over** a cold.*

* This meaning of **To get over** always takes an object. This is not necessarily the case with **To recover**.

ii. (To resolve, overcome a problem, difficulty)

Examples:
- We **got over** the problem of sacking him by encouraging him to give in his notice instead.
- I don't want to keep picking you up on everything, but how do your plans **get over** our cash-flow difficulties?

iii. (To believe)

Examples:
- I called on John this morning and I couldn't **get over** how filthy his place was.
- She can't **get over** the fact that I told her she's just not cut out for this type of job.

This meaning is generally used in the negative, after **can't** or **couldn't** to express surprise.

iv. (To make oneself/one's opinions understood, to be able to communicate)

Examples:
- I agree that, in most areas, he's on the ball but his biggest problem is that he can't seem to **get** his views **over**.
- When it comes down to it, everything depends on whether she manages to **get** her message **over** to the shareholders.

Note that for this meaning of **To get over**, **To get** *across* and **To put over**/*across* can also be used.
One should also compare the use of **To get over** (and the words mentioned above) with **To come over** (see Page 12). They have the same meaning but require a different construction,

e.g. 1. *She got her message over to the shareholders.*
(message = object)
  2. *Her message came over to the shareholders.*
(message = subject)

To get something over with/out of the way (to finish a task as soon as possible so that one has more time to do more pleasant/easier things)

Examples:
- A: Shall we have a go at preparing this
          follow-up document this morning?
  B: Well I suppose we might as well
          get it over with/out of the way.
- I can't wait to* **get** these exams **over with/out of the way**;
  they're driving me up the wall.

* i.e. *I'm really looking forward to getting...*

*"I shouldn't bother taking me on if I were you; my tennis is very **dodgy**."*

(see Page 78)

Lesson Three

To take up

i. (To start a hobby, sport etc.)

Examples:
- A: *I'd like to **take up** swimming when the children break up (from school).*
  B: *I bet you won't keep it up.*
- *If you are as bored as you make out, why don't you **take up** something like learning a foreign language?*

ii. (To become a resident, i.e. to take up residence)

Example:
- *He has applied to **take up** residence in Switzerland, but they are bound to turn him down.*

iii. (To occupy space or time)

Examples:
- *Your computer will **take up** almost the entire desk. How come you didn't get a smaller one?*
- *I'm sorry to bother you but I promise I won't **take up** much of your time.*

iv. (To consult, discuss a problem with a person/people who is/are also concerned with that matter)

Examples:
- *The Board of Directors must work out how the company is going to get over the problem of middle management, before they **take** it **up** with the shareholders.*
- *Before you leave, I have quite a number of matters I'd like to **take up** with you.*

One would not use this meaning of **To take up** to express the idea of discussing problems in general with one's friends or family. The person being spoken to in the second example is probably professionally involved with the speaker's problems (e.g. lawyer, bank manager etc.).

v. (To accept an offer or invitation)

Examples:
- *I wish I could have afforded to turn his offer down*
  *but, due to my huge overdraft, I reluctantly **took** it **up**.*
- A: *You must come round to dinner next time you're in town.*
- B: *Thank you. I'll **take** you **up** on that.**

*When used in relation to an invitation, To take someone up on something is normally an acceptance of a general invitation rather than one with a specific time and date.

To make fun of (To laugh *at* someone, to tease, make jokes about someone)

Examples:
- *I was always **made fun of** at school because I was so clumsy.*
- *Don't **make fun of** my pronunciation! It's not that* dreadful.*

* See **Posh** (Page 11).

Row, to row

i. (An argument, quarrel, to argue, quarrel with someone)

Examples:
- *I had an appalling **row** with my mother*
  last week and I still haven't got over it.
- *Most of his time is taken up by **rowing** with his partners.*

Note that for this meaning, the pronunciation of the **o** is long, as in **cow** or **now**. This should not be confused with the verb **to row** (a boat) which is pronounced with a short **o**, as in **go**.

ii. (A number of chairs, people, etc. arranged in a horizontal line)

Examples:
- *I hope it's not putting you out, but the only*
  *seats we have left are in the front **row**.*
- A: *I really can't keep up with her;*
      where on earth has she got to now?
- B: *I think I can make her out over there,*
      *behind that **row** of policemen.*

Pronunciation as in **To row** (a boat).
Note also the expression in a row/running/on the trot which means one after the other or, consecutively,
e.g.   1.   I've gone off that restaurant but maybe it's because I've been there
           three Saturdays **in a row/on the trot**.
       2.   Even though we've been to Greece two years **running/on the trot**,
           we're really looking forward to going back there again this summer.

To get by (To survive/manage on a small amount of something, e.g. money, sleep, knowledge)

Examples:

- *I **get by** on what I earn but, now the interest rates have been put up, I could do with a better salary.*
- *It's unheard of for my grandmother to stay in bed until lunchtime. She normally **gets by** on four hours sleep a night.*
- *My French is very dodgy, but I can just about **get by** in* German.*

* Note that **in** is always used before a language.

To call it a day (To finish a day's work, meeting, etc.)

Examples:

- *I think we may as well **call it a day** now; the meeting has gone on for over three hours.*
- *Let's **call it a day**; we can pick up where we left off tomorrow.*

Although this expression is generally used in the sense of finishing something for the time being only (rather than forever), it is sometimes employed as an informal way of saying to retire,

e.g. *I don't think John is up to working any more. It's about time he **called it a day**.*

To run over

i. (To go over)

Examples:

- *You ought to **run over** the contract just once more to check that there are no mistakes which you have failed to pick up.*
- *You'd better listen carefully because I'm not going to **run over** it again.*

See Page 12. For this meaning of **To run over** we could also use To run *through*.

ii. (To hit or pass over a person, animal or object with a motor vehicle)

Examples:

- *He said that he was going to sue the lorry driver who **ran over** his dog.*
- A: *How come you're so late?*
- B: *I got a puncture.*
  *I must have **run over** a broken bottle in the road.*

Cross (angry)

Example:

- *I don't want to have a row with you but I'm so **cross** that you let him get away with it again.*

83

Odd

i. (Strange)

Examples:

- *I don't know why we took on such an **odd** character.*
  He's not cut out for this type of work at all.
- *How **odd**! I'm sure I was meant to pick him up*
  at the airport, but he hasn't turned up.

Note the expression Oddly enough which means *It's interesting you should say that because...,*
e.g.   A: *I haven't seen Anna for ages.*
        B: ***Oddly enough**, I bumped into her only the other day.*

ii. (The opposite of even numbers, i.e. those numbers that cannot be divided by two)

Example:

- *The row of houses on this side of the road have all got **odd** numbers.*

iii. (Occasional)

Examples:

- *My dad, who is retired, does the **odd** job now and again*
  but, these days, he can't really be bothered.
- *We do get the **odd** complaint, but most people don't like to make a fuss.*

iv. (Various, different kinds – often used with *jobs* or *things*)

Examples:

- *My brother will help you do up your flat;*
  *he's always doing **odd*** jobs around the house.*
- *You can try your dress on in the little room but be careful*
  *not to trip over all the **odd** things that are lying on the floor.*
- *I took the trouble to write down some **odd** points which I'd*
  like to take up with our solicitor.

* Compare this example with **iii.**, first example (above). Odd jobs generally relate to manual work (i.e. repairing, building) done at home and is used in the plural. The odd job, on the other hand, can be any type of work which is only done occasionally and is used in the singular after **the**.

v.   (Not a matching pair)

   Example:
   - Wife to husband:
     It's bad enough that your shirt doesn't go with your jacket,
     but I'm not letting you go out with **odd** *socks on.*

Note the expression The odd one out which means different from all the others,
   e.g.   *I felt* **the odd one out** *because I was the only one dressed in a suit, and everyone made fun of me.*

vi.   (Approximately, a little more than)

   Example:
   - *I was about to call the party off,*
     when twenty* **odd** *people turned up out of the blue.*

* Generally used for numbers greater than ten.

Odds

i.   (The chances, probability of winning, being successful)

   Examples:
   - *Please be straightforward with me.*
     What are the **odds** *on my daughter passing this exam?*
   - *The* **odds** *are* that they'll try it on,*
     even though they know they won't get away with it.

* i.e. It is likely that.

ii.   (Contrary to expectation, everyone's prediction)

   Examples:
   - *All the* **odds** *were against her.* She had neither*
     experience nor qualifications, but they still took her on.
   - *He hasn't really got over his wife's death but he manages*
     to get by in the face of incredible/against all (the) **odds**.

Note the expressions It makes no odds and To be at odds with. The first one means it doesn't make any difference; it doesn't matter to someone which thing is done or chosen,
   e.g.   **It makes no odds** *to me if we swap rooms.*
The second expression means to be in disagreement or on bad terms with someone,
   e.g.   *When he's not rowing with his mother over the state of his room,*
            he's **at odds with** *her for some other reason.*
* i.e. Nothing was in her favour; her chances were not very good.

To rule out (To deny the possibility of something bad/unpopular happening, to exclude someone/oneself from taking part in a particular activity)

Examples:

- *We know that the idea of redundancies does not go down well with the staff but we can't **rule out** the possibility of it happening.*
- *It's true that everyone's at odds with him but, as he is a director of the company, we can't afford to **rule** him **out** of any decision making.*
- *The captain has **ruled** himself **out** of tonight's match because he still hasn't got over the flu, which he came down with last month.*

To turn to

i. (To ask, to depend on someone for help when one is in a desperate situation, to become dependent on something – e.g. drugs, alcohol, etc.)

Examples:

- *If you think you're not going to be able to cope, I want you to know that you can always **turn to** us.*
- *She's so depressed at the moment. The odds are that she'll **turn to** alcohol again.*

ii. (To deal with/consider a new matter, subject in a formal discussion or speech, to ask people to consider a matter)

Examples:

- *Before we call it a day, I wish to **turn to** the important matter of company finance.*
- *I'd like now to **turn** (your minds) **to** the subject of pollution in our cities and then I'll go on to discuss the environment in general.*

*"Please be straightforward with me. What are the **odds** on my daughter passing this exam?"*

(see Page 85)

TEACHER and STUDENTS

TEACHER: *I think it's best to* get *the homework* over *with first, then we can* pick up where
            we left off *last lesson.*

            I thought that this class was more on the ball *than Class B but it's quite apparent
            that it's* the other way round. *I don't enjoy* having a go *at you, but your homework
            was appalling. I think my problem is that I've let you all* get away with murder
            during most of the year and now it's too late to hope that your work will pick
            up *before the exams. Anyway, I'm sorry to* fly off the handle *at you like this,
            but something has to be done* to get *my message* across. It makes no odds *to me
            whether you pass your exams or not; it's entirely up to you.*

            Let's just run over *some of the questions. I'd like the girls to give me their answers
            to all the* odd *questions and the boys can handle the even ones.*

DAVID: *I can't remember the answers; I'll just have to* make *them* up *if I'm asked.*

TEACHER: *Right, the girl sitting in the third* row *behind John, what's your name?*

BARBARA: *Barbara.*

TEACHER: *Oh yes of course. Barbara, what was your answer to the first question,
            "Which king came after George III?"*

BARBARA: *George II.*

TEACHER: *Do you know, that's such a stupid answer I can't even be bothered to get annoyed.
            Didn't you* pick up *anything in your mathematics classes?
            I can understand people making the* odd *mistake but how on earth can George II
            come after George III?*

JANE: *Poor Barbara, she's always being* made fun of *by the teachers.*

CATHY: *I can't* get over *how slow she is to catch on. What are the* odds on *her ever
            getting a question right?*

JANE: *I've no idea, but there doesn't seem to be anyone she can* turn to *for help. She's
            constantly* at odds with *her parents, who didn't* take up *the headmaster's
            invitation to come up to the school to discuss her problems.*

TEACHER: *Jane, instead of talking, perhaps you could give me the correct answer.*

JANE: *Was it George IV, Sir?*

TEACHER: *Brilliant! But it still doesn't* make up for *all the other questions you got wrong. Now who would like to* have a go *at answering Question 2? David perhaps?*

DAVID: How come *I always get the difficult ones?*

TEACHER: *How was Queen Victoria related to William IV?*

DAVID: *Pardon?*

TEACHER: *Don't* make out *you didn't hear the question. Just* have a go.

DAVID: *She was his mother.*

TEACHER: *Do you know, this class is* driving me up the wall. *If Queen Victoria succeeded William IV to the throne, how could she have been his mother?*

DAVID: *Why do you always* pick *me* up *on every little mistake I make?*

TEACHER: *Because you have failed three history papers* in a row *and the* odds *are that you'll fail in the Summer too.*

DAVID: *I think I'll* get by *in life without being a history professor.*

TEACHER: *Well, one thing I can say is that you're not the* odd one out *in this class. You're all as thick as each other!*

[The bell rings for break-time]:

TEACHER: *Let's* call it a day *but there are some* odd *points I'd like to* run through *next time.*

INTERVIEWER: *I'd like now to* turn to *the question of tax rises. A lot of us in the media can't* make out *the Government's policy on this. Are they coming? If so, when?*

P/MINISTER: *There are no immediate plans to increase taxes, but we can't* rule out *the possibility in the future. I'll be* taking up *the matter* with *my colleagues in the Cabinet within the next few weeks but I'd like to* pick up *on a point you raised earlier. This country has survived a severe recession* against all the odds, *and now we have to* make up *our minds as to whether we want to lead the industrial world once again. We have to* turn *mere survival* into *economic success, and I believe we've got the potential.*

INTERVIEWER: *Some people find it* odd *that we have only two months* to go *before the European Elections and the Government still haven't* got over *the problem of who is going to* make up *the various committees on European health and education.*

P/MINISTER: *As you know, we've had rather a* hectic *domestic schedule lately, but without wishing to* dodge *the question, we shall let the press know of any news concerning this matter in due course.*

INTERVIEWER: *Prime Minister, thank you for allowing us to* take up *your valuable time.*

Dear Tracy,

So sorry I haven't written for quite a while but I'm off to France next week to see my cousin Peter; so, thing's have been a little hectic. On top of that, I've picked up the flu and have been trying to get over it for about a month. In fact, to be perfectly honest, my life has been upside down recently. I've split up with Justin (again). I should have listened to you in the first place. You're quite right, he's definitely a dodgy character. My problem is that I was so much in love with him that whenever he was nasty, I let him off. Anyway, I'm sure he was picking up other women or at least trying it on with them when I wasn't keeping an eye on him. Everyone says we're bound to make up because we've had so many rows in the past, but this time it really is all over.

To change the subject; Peter has decided to take up residence in France. I can't get over it! Can you imagine that Peter, who likes to drink his English beer in one go, is going to become French? Whilst I was there, he was picked up for speeding and he made up some story that I was about to have a baby. He hasn't changed!

One more thing: are you coming over this Christmas or are you going to put it off once again? Sorry to keep going on at you, but you are bound to miss a great time if you don't turn up. Get back to me on this as soon as you can, because my parents want me to tell them if it will be necessary to put you up. If you do come over, you'll have to pick up all my parents' bills and you can make the cheque out to me (only joking!).

All my love,

Jane

Chapter Four: **Exercise**

CHOOSE THE CORRECT WORD FROM THOSE IN BLUE
Answers on page 204.

DRIVING INSTRUCTOR and STUDENT:

INSTRUCTOR: *Tell me David, have you done any practising since we last met?*

STUDENT: *Yes, I went out with my dad on Sunday but we had a terrible
[1](shout/row/go/holiday). He had a [2](go/fight/argument/hit) at me for
driving too near the parked cars and I [3](took/fly/pulled/flew) off the
[4](door/floor/wall/ handle). Even though it was Sunday, I wasn't able to
[5](dodge/get/break/forget) the traffic. It was really [6](lively/lovely/hectic/sunny);
I couldn't get [7](off/over/at/out) how many cars were on the road.
Anyway, we [8](broke/took/made/did) up soon after.*

INSTRUCTOR: *Well, I hope you're feeling on the [9](ball/game/mood/ready) today, because we're
going to practise in a busy area. This is the best way to [10](catch/do/pick/take)
up driving skills.*

STUDENT: *I think I'm more likely to be [11](arrested/picking/stood/picked) up by the police
for my driving skills! Be honest: what are the [12](probability/odds/chance/luck)
on my passing this test?*

INSTRUCTOR: *Quite high if you listen to my advice. Now you have to remember, don't allow
yourself to get [13](cross/sad/anger/annoy) with other drivers and don't worry too
much about the rules. If you're at [14](odds/home/pressure/agreement) with the
Highway Code, I will soon tell you. Now, I'd like you to drive up to the traffic lights
and turn left.*

STUDENT: *That seems straightforward enough. Oh no! I'm in the wrong lane.
How [15](can/come/could/why) I can never get in the right position?*

INSTRUCTOR: *Be careful! You can't just move over without looking in your mirror.*

STUDENT: *Oh dear. Maybe I should never have taken [16](off/up/out/in) driving in the first
place.*

INSTRUCTOR: *Don't be ridiculous. When you wish to change positions in the road, you have to
[17](do/open/pick/make) up your mind where you want to go, check in your mirror
if anything is coming, signal and then move.*

STUDENT: *You know, it's [18](odd/odds/unusual/different): every time I come to this area, I
have difficulties. I have now been here four Fridays in a
[19](line/together/row/month). Can't we go somewhere else for a change?*

INSTRUCTOR: *Stop talking and concentrate on the road.*

[15 minutes later]

INSTRUCTOR: *You do realise you've just gone through a red light? It's OK as a learner to do these things; you can ²⁰(get/take/go/make) away with ²¹(somebody/killing/nothing/murder) but once you've passed your test, the police won't let you ²²(out/off/up/win). Am I ²³(telling/making/driving/getting) my message ²⁴(over/around/with/at) to you?*

STUDENT: *Yes, I'm sorry, but the bloke on my right was trying it ²⁵(up/in/on/out). He wanted to pass in front of me.*

INSTRUCTOR: *That's no excuse for missing a red light. Now why don't you ²⁶(have/make/try/play) a go at reversing around a corner?*

STUDENT: *Well I suppose we might as well as get it ²⁷(off/over/out/about) with.*

INSTRUCTOR: *Now try not to ²⁸(build/get/bring/take) up the whole road when you stop... That's it... Good!*

STUDENT: *Can you run ²⁹(up/out/over/in) what I have to do again?*

INSTRUCTOR: *No! We've done it twenty ³⁰(odds/odd/strange/enough) times already. Remember to check in your mirror before reversing... That was good. Now let's ³¹(call/give/make/say) it a ³²(end/year/day/drive). We can ³³(get/pick/speak/take) up where we left ³⁴(on/at/about/off) next week.*

STUDENT: *Just one thing. Who do I ³⁵(give/take/make/pass) the cheque out to?*

INSTRUCTOR: *Best Driving School.*

JANICE: *Hello, Pat, how are you?*

PAT: *Still trying to get* [36]*(over/round/out/off) a cold.*

JANICE: *I must say, you seem to* [37]*(take/bring/pick/make) up colds quite regularly*

PAT: *Yes I know. I catch them from the kids....... How are you doing?*

JANICE: *Well, we're* [38]*(on/off/go/take) to Italy next Sunday. John only gets the* [39]*(seldom/occasionally/one/odd) chance to get away; so we thought we might as well take the opportunity. He makes* [40]*(out/on/off/up) that holidays mean nothing to him but he always enjoys himself once he's there. How's your boy? I notice he has* [41]*(become/turned/made/changed) into a handsome young man.*

PAT: *Oh, thank you. Well, he's only got two weeks to go before he goes off to university, but I can't* [42]*(have/take/make/understand) out what he's going to study there. Anyway, it's something to do with computers. And your kids? If I remember rightly, John was working in a supermarket and Steve was training to become a policeman.*

JANICE: *No actually, it's the other way* [43]*(up/out/off/round).*

PAT: *Oh, yes of course, how silly of me! Oh look, there's Vivian's daughter and who's that with her?*

JANICE: *It must be a new man she's* [44]*(met/taken/picked/got) up. She seems to change them every week.*

PAT: *Apparently she used to turn* [45]*(up/to/towards/away) her last boyfriend for money until it* [46]*(caused/made/drove/took) him round the* [47]*(bend/road/straight/corner).*

JANICE: *Well, that's interesting. I was meaning to ask you: does your husband still do* [48]*(good/many/various/odd) jobs? It's just that one of our doors is a bit* [49]*(unfortunate/dodgy/closed/useful) and has nearly come off its hinges.*

PAT: *Oh yes of course. He'd be delighted to help. The only problem is that he has pulled a muscle in his right leg and has had to* [50]*(take/rule/call/get) himself out of all sport and exercise for a couple of weeks. He has promised to* [51]*(try/take/bring/make) it up to his five-a-side football team next month but, I must say, he seems to be* [52]*(getting/give/picking) up already.*

JANICE: *Well, there's no hurry. Anyway, I must be off. See you soon.*

Lesson One

Fun (A good time, enjoyable)

Examples:
- *What a great weekend! I haven't had so much **fun** in ages.*
- A: *How did your dinner party turn out?*
  B: *Oh, it was great **fun**.*

Funny

i. (Amusing, humorous, someone or something who/which makes one laugh)

Examples:
- *Not only is he on the ball when it comes to business but he's also a very **funny** man socially.*
- *We had such a **funny** weekend; I haven't laughed so much in ages.**

* Compare with "Fun" (See first example above). That sentence meant that the weekend was enjoyable because many interesting and entertaining things happened. This example (**funny**), however, means that a good time was had because many amusing things happened that made one laugh.

ii. (Strange, unusual)

Examples:
- *It's a **funny** situation; I don't really know who to take the matter up with.*
- *She's gone off the idea of travelling around the world because she's a bit **funny*** about flying.*
- *One minute she's making a fuss of you and the next she's making a fuss about you. She really is a **funny** person!°*

Note the expression Funnily enough which is a more common way of saying **oddly enough** (see Page 84),
　　　e.g. A: *Have you heard from Jane lately?*
　　　　　B: ***Funnily enough**, she's off to university tomorrow.*
Also note the expression I have a funny feeling (that) which means **I'm afraid/I suspect (that)**,
　　　e.g. *I've a **funny feeling** (that) she won't turn up tonight.*
* This is a very colloquial way of saying, *she's very nervous/fussy about flying.*
° Simply reading this sentence does not tell us whether the speaker thinks the woman is strange or amusing. It often depends on the intonation and facial expression of the speaker. Also, if **Funny** is preceded by the words **a bit**, it usually means strange. If the listener cannot understand if the speaker means strange or amusing, he or she can simply ask the question,
　　　*Do you mean funny **peculiar** or funny **ha-ha**?*

To get through

i.   (To manage to speak to someone on the telephone because the line is not busy)

Examples:

- *Yesterday, I made up my mind to call John but
I couldn't **get through** (to him).**
- *I can't seem to **get through** at the moment.
Would you° mind having a go?*

* I can't/couldn't get through simply means the line is engaged.

° **You** in this sentence should be pronounced emphatically. It suggests that the speaker has done all he can without success and it may be different if the other person tries.

ii.   (To succeed in making someone understand something)

Examples:

- *He's not thick but he's very difficult to **get through** to/
it's very difficult to **get through** to him.*
- *She keeps telling him to stop nagging her, but
the message doesn't seem to be **getting through** (to him).*

iii.   (To manage to survive a difficult period of time, to complete a lot of work)

Examples:

- *I don't know how I **got through** last week.
I felt all the odds were against me.*
- *I've just been running over her finances, and it's quite apparent
that she'll have problems in **getting through*** next year.*
- *I'll never **get through** all this work by lunch time;
it's bound to take up the whole day.*

* Compare with **To get by** (see Page 83). Even though they are very similar in meaning, **To get** *through* is more concerned with the completion of a specific period of time, whilst **To get** *by* emphasises survival during that period. In addition, **To get through** must be followed by a period of time,

e.g.   *I earn just enough money* **to get by/to get through** *the month*.

iv.   (To pass an exam, to win a round in a competition)

Examples:

- *Fifty odd students took the exam but only eight **got through**.*
- *Although Liverpool put up a brave fight, Manchester United won the
match which means they have **got through*** to the semi-finals for
the second year in a row.*

* We could also say *Manchester United* are *through*.

v.   (To use up,* consume, spend – e.g. food, clothes, money)

Examples:
- In a restaurant:
  *I won't be able to **get through** all of this food.*
  Do you mind if we swap dishes?
- *I can't get over how many shoes you've **got through** this year.°*
- *I must cut down on spending. It's only Monday and I've
  already **got through** a hundred pounds.*

* Note that one cannot ask, tell or advise someone **To get through** something in the sense of using it up; i.e. one
would **not** say *Can you get through this milk, otherwise it will go off?*
° With clothes, **To get through** is usually used in the plural and means to wear out; i.e. one would **not** say *I've **got
through** this shirt* but instead one could say *I've **got through** three shirts this month.*

vi.   (To be approved officially by an authority – e.g. parliament, a committee)

Example:
- *The odds on his latest proposals **getting through** Parliament
  are very slim.** (see picture below)

* i.e. unlikely.

To get hold of

i. (To manage to speak to someone on the telephone because they are there, to be able to contact someone)

Examples:

- *Yesterday I made up my mind to call John but I couldn't **get hold of*** him.*
- *You're so difficult to **get hold of** these days.° What are you up to?*

* Compare with **To get through** (see Page 95). That example meant that the caller could not speak to John because the line was engaged, whilst in this example, **To get hold of,** the caller cannot communicate with John because he is not at home or in the office,

e.g. *When I finally succeeded in **getting through**, your secretary couldn't get hold of you.*

° This means that the person is never at home, in the office etc.

ii. (To manage to obtain something)

Examples:

- *I'll ask round the office but I can tell you now that tickets for a Wimbledon final are almost impossible to **get hold of**.*
- *Things are a bit hectic today, but I'll try and **get hold of** the keys to the flat so that you can go round to see it tonight.*

iii. (To come to a certain conclusion, to get an impression – usually the wrong one)

Examples:

- *I don't know where you **got** (**hold of**) the idea that we were prepared to take up your offer.*
- *It's very odd. How on earth could he have **got hold of** such an impression?*

Note the expression To get (hold of) the wrong end of the stick which means to misunderstand someone or something. It is often used in relation to instructions, a set of facts or where someone has taken offence where none was intended,

e.g.   1.   *I was under the impression that the bank was going to put up at least 50% of the capital, but I must have **got (hold of) the wrong end of the stick**.*

2.   A: *I'm sorry, I won't stand for that sort of rudeness!*
     B: *I was only joking. You've **got (hold of) the wrong end of the stick**.*

Daunting, to be daunted (A frightening or worrying thought, task, to be frightened by, afraid of)

Examples:
- *The fact they are unlikely to get through the work on time is a rather **daunting** thought.*
- *Having to put up another hundred thousand pounds is quite a **daunting** prospect.*
- *Bringing up children is a **daunting** task these days.*
- *Even though they had never got through the opening rounds of the competition, they weren't **daunted** by the opposition they had to take on.*

To look up (To search for a word, telephone number, or other piece of information in a book, e.g. dictionary, address book)

Examples:
- *I can't usually be bothered to **look up** the meaning of words in the dictionary. I just go on with what I'm reading.*
- *I haven't got her number handy. I'll have to **look** it **up** in my phone book at home and get back to you with it tomorrow.*

Note the expression Things are looking up which means things look like they are going to improve,

    e.g.   *We may still need to call on your help, but **things are** (**definitely**) **looking up**.*

To look up to (To respect, admire someone)

Examples:
- *Funnily enough, I'm the only one in this office who doesn't **look up to** him.*
- *I **look up to** my father even though I'm always rowing with him.*

This expression is generally used for someone one knows well who is usually older and more experienced. The opposite of **To look up** *to* is To look down on i.e. To think that someone is inferior. It is not just restricted to people one knows,

    e.g.   *He's so stuck-up; I won't stand for the way he **looks down on** my family.*

No wonder ("It isn't surprising that something bad happened")

Examples:
- A: *I've got through two loaves of bread this week.*
  B: ***No wonder*** *you're getting fat!*
- *(It's)* ***no wonder*** *she's unhappy;*
  she's got no one to turn to in these situations.

It's a wonder obviously means *It's surprising that something **good** happened.*

e.g. 1.   *It's a wonder they are still partners after the terrible rows they keep on having.*
2.   *He's so careless with money; it's a wonder that he can get by.*

To dread (To fear, to be frightened of something that is going to/may happen in the future, to have a great desire not to do something)

Examples:
- A: *Why are you frowning so much?*
  B: *I'm sorry, I can't help it;*
  *I just **dread** going* into work at the moment.*
- *To tell you the truth, I **dread** Christmas.*
  I can't cope with all the family reunions.
- *She **dreaded** that he would go up the wall*
  if he ever caught on to what was going on.

* If used with a verb, it is *usually* the gerund which follows the verb **To dread** rather than the infinitive. However, one should note the expression I dread to think which means **I don't want to imagine**,

e.g. 1.   *I dread to think what the world would be like if the Nazis got hold of power again.*
2.   A: *What do you believe will happen if he doesn't get away with it?*
   B: *I dread to think!*

Flop, to flop

i.   (A failure, not a commercial success, to fail, be unsuccessful –
especially a film, play, plan etc.)

Examples:
- *Even though the play got over its initial problems,*
  *it turned out to be a complete **flop** in the end.*
- *The partners of the company turned down his offer to reshape the*
  *business because they thought the whole scheme would **flop**.*

ii.   (To fall heavily onto/into something –
usually a bed or armchair when one is tired)

Example:
- *After a hectic day in the office, I like to **flop** into an armchair*
  and be made a fuss of.

To drop off

i. (To stop in order to let someone out of a car, to take someone somewhere by car)

Examples:
- Taxi driver:
  It looks like we're going to be held up for quite a while.
  *Would you like to be **dropped** (**off**) somewhere else?*
- *Would it be putting you out if you **dropped** me (**off**) at the airport?*

Compare this use of **To drop off** with **To pick up** (see Page 74).

ii. (To fall asleep – often by accident for a short while)

Examples:
- *I **dropped off** right in the middle of the meeting;*
  I felt quite awkward when I woke up.
- *She won't ask us round again if you keep*
  ***dropping off** whilst her husband is talking to you.*

iii. (To decrease in demand, to decline – usually in business or public interest)

Examples:
- *Business has **dropped off** a little but*
  it's bound to pick up by the summer.
- *Interest in taking up the Government's share offers has*
  ***dropped off** dramatically in recent months.*

Chapter Five

Lesson Two

To rate (To consider someone/something as being important – often used with the word "highly", to have a high opinion of someone or something)

> Examples:
> * *Dedication and a spotless reputation are* ***rated*** *very highly in this profession.*
> * *I can't make out why everyone* ***rates***** him as an accountant; he can hardly add up!*

If we say that someone or something is Overrated, it means that people give this person or thing more value and respect than he/it really deserves,

> e.g.   *Everyone keeps going on about how funny that film is. I think it's* ***overrated****.*

On the contrary, if someone or something is Underrated, it means the subject ought to be valued more highly,

> e.g.   *I think his potential is* ***underrated****. We could really do with a person like him in this firm.*

* When used in the *active voice* **To rate** is considered to be more *colloquial*.

To rave about/over (To get excited about something because of its high quality, to have a *very* high opinion of something) **Colloquial**

> Examples:
> * *John, my partner, is very happy about last year's turnover, but I don't think it's anything to* ***rave about/over****.*
> * *He's always* ***raving about/over*** *English pubs, but I think they're overrated.*

Therefore, **To rave about/over** can be a more emphatic way of saying **To rate** (See example above).
Note also that a Rave-review is an article in the press, which praises very highly a particular performance, film etc,

> e.g.   *Even though the show received* ***rave-reviews*** *in most of the newspapers, it flopped.*

"I can't make out why everyone ***rates*** *him as an accountant; he can hardly add up!"*

Hassle, to hassle (A nuisance, problem, inconvenient, to cause someone inconvenience) **Slang**

Examples:
- *First I had to drop my mother off at the post office,*
  then I spent hours trying to get through to my bank manager
  *and finally I was held up in traffic. What a **hassle**!*
- *I could do without you **hassling*** me;*
  I promise I'll do it when I get the odd moment.
- *There's nothing that drives me up the wall more than*
  *a shop assistant **hassling** me to try on clothes*
  as soon as I enter his store.

* This use of **To hassle** is very similar in meaning and usage to **To nag** (See Page 61).

To fancy

i. (To feel like or be in the mood for doing/having something) **Colloquial**

Examples:
- *I **fancy** going to the sales this afternoon*
  to see if we can pick up some bargains.
- *It's a pity you're not up to going out today;*
  *I really **fancy** a drive in the country.*

ii. (To be sexually attracted to someone) **Colloquial**

Examples:
- *He **fancies** every pretty woman he meets, but*
  looks don't rate very highly as far as I'm concerned.
- *He looks down on any woman who doesn't **fancy** him.*

Note the expression To fancy oneself which means that a person has a very high opinion of himself/herself,
  e.g. *No wonder everybody has gone off him; he **fancies himself** far too much.*

iii. ("What a surprise!") **Colloquial**

Examples:
- A: *I bumped into our old headmaster last week.*
  B: ***Fancy** that!*
- ***Fancy** seeing you here! I thought you had taken up residence in Spain.*
- ***Fancy** telling her she was thick!* No wonder she's so upset.*

Note the expression To fancy one's chances which means to have great hope in succeeding. It is often used in the negative,
  e.g. *I don't really **fancy my chances** of getting the job; the odds against me are too high.*
* i.e. Why on earth did you tell her she was thick?

I could murder (+ food/drink) (To have a great desire to eat or drink something in particular) **Colloquial**

Examples:
- *I've had such a hectic day;* **I could murder** *a cup of tea.*
- A: *Do you fancy a Chinese take-away?*
  B: *No, not really, but* **I could murder** *a pizza.*

To pick on (To treat someone differently to others in an unfair way – either verbally or physically)

Examples:
- *I don't know why the boss is* **picking on** *me lately.*
  Why doesn't he have a go at someone else for a change?
- *You've got the wrong end of the stick.*
  I didn't mean to **pick on** *you; it's just the way it came across.*
- *When I was a young boy at school, I was often* **picked on**
  by the bigger pupils because I was always the odd one out.

Note the position of the person or pronoun is different from most phrasal verbs, in that it comes after the preposition.
   e.g.   *Don't pick on me!*
          and **not** *Don't pick me on!*
Compare with *I'll be round to pick* **you** *up...* (see Page 74).

To run out

i.   (To have nothing left of something, to get used up)

Examples:
- A: *We're* **running out** *of petrol/The petrol is* **running out**.
  B: *It serves you right! I told you to fill up over an hour ago.*
- *I thought I'd be able to put up with the situation but*
  I've **run out** *of patience/my patience has* **run out**.

Compare these two sentences: *I've run* **out** *of money* and
                               I'm running **short** *of money.*

ii.   (To expire, become invalid)

Examples:
- *I'm so cross with you; you knew your visa was*
  running out *but you couldn't be bothered to renew it.*
- *I didn't realise my bus pass had* **run out**.
  I was lucky to be let off.

To take in

i.   (To listen, and absorb information)

Examples:
- Teacher to student:
  *You didn't **take in** a word I said last lesson;*
  I might as well not have taught you.
- *Fancy expecting her to **take in** all that information in one go!**

* i.e. *It was too much to ask her to absorb all that information at once.*

ii.   (To deceive, to trick someone)

Examples:
- *She wasn't **taken in** by the salesman who*
  tried to sell her a dodgy washing machine.
- *I can't get over how you let him **take** you **in** like that.*

A person who is easily taken in may be described as being gullible, i.e. a person who believes everything he is told,

e.g.   *Her brother might be **easily taken in**, but she is not quite so **gullible**.*

To come along

i.   (To appear, present oneself, itself – usually unexpectedly)

Examples:
- *After his marriage broke up,*
  he went out with the first girl that **came along**.*
- *Even though we are short of staff at the moment,*
  we can't afford to take on just anyone that **comes along**.*
- *A rave-review like this doesn't **come along** very often.*

* This meaning is often used with **the first** or **anyone**.

ii.   (To hurry up – usually imperative)*

Example:
- ***Come along**! We're running out of time.*

iii.   (To accompany someone)

Examples:
- *I gather that you're going to take on John at tennis next week.*
  *Would you mind if I **came along** and watched?*
- *We're going over to Jane's this evening.*
  *Why don't you **come along** as well?*

iv.   (To progress, develop)*

Examples:
- *How are your plans for the new company **coming**° **along**?*
  It sounds like a daunting task to me.
- *She was a bit slow to catch on when she first started but*
  *now she's **coming**° **along** fine.*

* Note that **To come on** could also be used only for meanings **ii.** and **iv.**
° Generally used in the Present Progressive form and not in the negative.

Biased

i.   (Partial, one-sided, showing personal prejudice)

Examples:
- *Of course you don't think your brother*
  *picked on that little boy; you're **biased**!*
- *The judge is bound to be **biased** in favour of/towards**
  the second defendant because they belong to the same rugby club.
- *It is quite apparent that the company is **biased** against* women.*

* Compare the constructions *Biased in favour of/towards* with *Biased against.*

ii.   (To specialise in certain subjects, areas more than others)

Example:
- *I gather that your firm of solicitors is **biased** towards company law/*
  *has a company law **bias**.**

* Note that in this example it would probably be more common to use the noun **bias** (i.e. the second construction).

105

Lesson Three

To get on

i. (To achieve a high position, to do well, to manage)

Examples:
- *If you want to* **get on** *in the business world, you have to be on the ball.*
- *I know your sister got through her exams, but how did you* **get on**?*

Compare with **To come along** (see Page 104).
* i.e. *How did you do?*

ii. (To become late or old, to approach – in time or age)

Examples:
- *It's time we were off; it's* **getting on**.
- *It must be* **getting on** *for 10 o'clock. Where on earth has she got to?*
- *Just because he's* **getting on** *a bit, (it) doesn't mean he should be allowed to get away with murder.*
- *Some of the directors who make up the Board are* **getting on** *for 80.*

To get on (well) with

i. (To have good relations with someone without disagreement or argument)

Examples:
- *Even though I look up to my mother, I don't really* **get on** (well) **with** *her.*
- *We used to* **get on** (very well **with** each other) *but now I dread bumping into her.*

ii. (To hurry up and finish something*, to go ahead and do something which requires attention and concentration, e.g. work)

Examples:
- *Instead of making a fuss, why don't you just* **get on with** *it?*
- *I really fancy going out tonight but unfortunately, I have to* **get on with** *some work.*

* Compare with **To go on** (see Page 17).
Get on with *what you're saying!* is much stronger and less polite than
Go on with *what you were saying!*
The first sentence (**Get on**) means *Hurry up!* whilst the second sentence (**Go on**) means *Continue!*

iii. (To pass the time doing something while waiting for the main thing to happen – "*to be* getting on with")

Examples:
- A: *Dinner's not quite ready, so here are a few snacks to be **getting on** with.**
  B: *Great! I could murder a sandwich.*
- *The meeting has had to be put off until 2pm, but I'm sure you all have plenty of things to be **getting on** with for the time being.*

* i.e. Why don't you start eating these snacks and by the time we have finished them, dinner will be ready?

To get on to (To contact someone – usually professional – in order to tell them to do/to find out something)

Examples:
- A. *How come the plumber didn't come round this morning?*
  B: *I don't know; I'll **get on to** him straight-away.*
- *We can't put up with this any longer. You'll have to **get on to** the accountant about it.*

To get on to is also a slightly more informal way of saying **To turn to** when relating to dealing with a particular subject (see Page 86).

Outcome (The result, consequence, conclusion)

Examples:
- *We may as well wait and see the **outcome** of the Board's discussions before we get on with any work.*
- *What was the **outcome** of that dreadful row the partners had last week?*

Uncalled-for (Behaviour or action which is unnecessary and without justification)

Examples:
- *Even though he has been getting to you recently, I think your behaviour towards him was totally **uncalled-for**.*
- *I think his sacking was **uncalled-for**; he's had to put up with a lot of hassle at home this year.*

To take over

i. (To take control of something – e.g. a company, conversation, country etc.)

Examples:
- *If ABC Ltd **take** us **over**, they're bound to be biased in favour of their own employees.*
- *I'd rather you didn't ask her round. You know what she's like; as soon as someone starts a conversation, she completely **takes over**.*
- *The Minister, who has been accused of racism, feels that people had got hold of the wrong end of the stick when he said that the country was being **taken over** by immigrants.*

Note that **To take over** can also be used as a noun (Take-over). For example, business people often talk about a **take-over bid** which is an offer to buy all the controlling shares of a particular company,

e.g. *Apparently, XYZ Ltd. turned down ABC's **take-over bid**.*

ii. (To take the place of someone)

Examples:
- *It makes no odds who **takes over** while you're away, as long as he's/she's competent.*
- *Lawyer to client:*
  *I've instructed my partner, Anna, to **take over** the case. Don't worry, I ran over all the details with her this morning.*

Mind you ("On the other hand", "but, I must say") **Colloquial**

Examples:
- *I think they're an appalling firm. **Mind you**, they have got an excellent accountant.*
- *I wouldn't swap my Rolls Royce for your Porsche. **Mind you**, I've always fancied the idea of having a sports car.*

To get carried away (To become too enthusiastic, involved or emotional about something without knowing when to stop)

Examples:
- *No wonder his wife left him; he got too **carried away** with his job.*
- *I understand why you had to tell him off but I thought you got a little bit **carried away**.*
- *I got a bit **carried away** with the shopping today. My wife is bound to hit the roof when she finds out how much money I've got through.*

To stick up for (To defend, support someone – usually verbally)

Examples:
- Just because he's my brother, it doesn't mean I'm going to **stick up for** him every time he gets into a row. It serves him right!
- Don't let him pick on you like that. **Stick up for** yourself!*

*When used in the reflexive form, it can mean to defend oneself physically as well as verbally.

To be/feel under the weather (To feel a little unwell)

Example:
- I'm sorry I'm having an off-day today but I'm **feeling** a little **under the weather**. Would you mind if I took the rest of the day off?

Sought-after (In demand, wanted)

Examples:
- Jobs in advertising are highly **sought-after** these days, but I'm not cut out for that particular lifestyle.
- He is meant to be one of the most **sought-after** footballers in Italy.

Note that **Sought** is the past of the verb To seek which means to look for, to search. **To be sought-after** is therefore the passive form of this verb.

"I got a bit **carried away** with the shopping today. My wife is bound to hit the roof when she finds out how much money I've got through." (see Page 108)

To show up (To embarrass someone in front of other people – the subject is usually a person with whom one has a close relationship)

Examples:
- Every time we have your father round to dinner with our neighbours, he **shows** us **up** (in front of them).
- Wife to husband:
  Can't you see that your tie doesn't go with your shirt?
  All the other men will be smart; please don't **show** me **up** by being the odd one out.

To show up also means the same as **To turn up** (see Page 15) and is probably more common in American English.

TELEPHONE CONVERSATION BETWEEN MOTHER AND DAUGHTER:

DAUGHTER: Hello, Mum. Who on earth have you been talking to all this time?
I've been trying to *get through to* you for ages.

MOTHER: I've been speaking to my friend, Patty.

DAUGHTER: You only saw her on Friday afternoon. Surely you must *run out* of things to say.

MOTHER: Well, the thing is, she has just realised she has been *taken in* by the man who sold
her her "new" car. You know how *gullible* she is. She just bought the first one that
came along. Apparently, he told her that it was one of the most *sought-after* cars
on the market.

DAUGHTER: What's wrong with it?

MOTHER: *Funnily enough*, everything! It's *a wonder* the car goes at all. Fixing it is going to
be a *daunting* task, but I told her to *get on* to Mike, the mechanic; *mind you*,
I dread to think what he's going to charge her.

DAUGHTER: Anyway, what have you been up to?

MOTHER: Well, last night your father and I *fancied* seeing a film. We managed to *get hold
of* tickets to see that Clint Eastwood one with Meryl Streep. It received
rave-reviews in all of the papers but we thought it was *overrated*. Actually,
I *dropped off* in the middle. After the film, your father said he could *murder
a hamburger* so we went to 'Jimmy's'. Dad was so hungry that while we were
waiting for our hamburgers he had some crisps to be *getting on with*. He really
showed me up; you know how Dad gets so *carried away with* his food.

DAUGHTER: You're always *picking on* him. *No wonder* he *dreads* going out to eat with you!

MOTHER: Oh, you're bound to *stick up for* him, being his daughter. You're *biased*...
Anyway, how are the kids?

DAUGHTER: Well, Jamie's been a bit *under the weather*, although I think his studies are *coming
along* well now. I just hope he's going to *get through* his exams. There's so much
information he needs to *take in*, it doesn't look *fun* at all. I *dropped* him *off* at
school the other day and he said to me he didn't know how he was going to *get
through* the next couple of weeks; but I told him that he *underrates* himself too
much and that if he wants to *get on* in this world, he must have confidence.
At last the message seems to be *getting through*.

MOTHER: Oh, good........ And the other one?

DAUGHTER: *Jane? She's fine. Last month she said her class mates were looking down on her because she got on so well with all her teachers.*

MOTHER: *I'm sure they're all jealous. She probably gets a lot of hassle from all the boys who fancy her.*

DAUGHTER: *She does; mind you, she's perfectly capable of sticking up for herself.*
Anyway, we're all dying to see you. Why don't you come over for dinner tonight?

MOTHER: *Well, I have a little bit of work to be getting on with but I'd love to see you and the kids. Is eight o'clock alright?*

DAUGHTER: *Fine.*

PARTNERS' MEETING:

SNR PARTNER: *It's getting on for seven o'clock. I think we should begin. Come along, let's all take our places. Now, I suppose everyone's aware of the takeover bid issued by Atlas Limited last week.*

PARTNER A: *Yes, but I don't fancy their chances of raising the capital before the offer period runs out. Apparently, business has dropped off in recent months.*

PARTNER B: *But things are looking up for us. There is a new Act which has just got through Parliament which protects the selling company when the purchaser can't raise the finance.*

PARTNER A: *Who cares what the Law says? If they don't have the money, the legal outcome is irrelevant. I knew this whole scheme would be a flop.*

SNR PARTNER: *I think your pessimism is uncalled for. I can't work out how you got hold of the idea that Atlas don't have any funds.*

PARTNER A: *I'm not so easily taken in. I know why their Managing Director is acting in such a funny way and is so difficult to get hold of these days. He can't cope with the hassle of taking over another company. Actually, I dread to think what will happen to us if he remains the head of Atlas.*

SNR PARTNER: *I think you've got hold of the wrong end of the stick. Why don't you all come along with me tomorrow to their offices and see what they have to say?*

Chapter Five: **Exercise**

CHOOSE THE CORRECT WORD FROM THOSE IN BLUE
Answers on page 205.

LETTER FROM BROTHER TO SISTER:

Dear Mary

I have given up trying to get [1](across/hold/through/about) to you on the phone so I thought I would write instead. I [2](dread/fear/afraid/scared) to think what your phone bill must be! Anyway I'd love to know how you [3](got/came/ went/did) on in your exams. I hope you didn't drop [4](out/in/off/by) in the middle, like you did a couple of years ago.

Last week I took Angela to see that film you were [5](raving/rating/over-rating/shouting) about, but both of us thought it was rather [6](excellent/poor/overrated/underrated). I felt the female character was too [7](appalling/incredible/sceptical/gullible). Even someone with her low intellect (the character, not Angela!) wouldn't have been [8](take/took/taken/ticking) in by that fool of a husband. [9](Telling/But/So/Mind) you, I couldn't really concentrate on the film because afterwards I knew I was going to be faced with the [10](wanting/worried/frightened/daunting) prospect of meeting Angela's parents for the first time.

[11](Funny/Strange/Funnily/Odd) enough, I got [12](up/on/at/in) better with her mother than her father, whose rude behaviour was [13](unnecessary/uncalled/called/appalling) for. He told me that Angela would marry the first rich boy that comes [14](around/along/up/with). He was obviously trying to drop me a hint that, knowing my low financial status, he didn't [15](like/agree/fancy/consider) my [16](chance/opportunity/probability/chances) of being Angela's husband. I thought no [17](wander/wonder/surprise/surprising) his children don't look [18](down/up/round/across) to him, if he [19](picks/put/shows/take) them up every time one of them brings a boyfriend home. Fortunately, Angela had warned me beforehand that her father was impossible to get [20](across/hold/over/through) to but that, when it came down to it, he had a kind heart. I must admit I didn't [21](like/want/fancy/wish) spending the rest of the evening with him, but things started to [22](come/bring/look/make) up when Angela's Mum suggested that we could have some [23](funny/fun/enjoyment/laugh) helping her to make a chocolate cake. She had [24](left/ran/run/work) out of butter and sent us to the shops while she got [25](away/off/on/through) with other things. Unfortunately, we got a bit [26](carried/taken/brought/thought) away and came back with a full bag of shopping. To be honest, I didn't realise that making a cake could involve so much [27](hassle/problem/difficulties/inconvenient), but the [28](outcome/results/end/consequence) made it worthwhile, and I have already decided that I now have the confidence to take [29](up/in/off/over) in the kitchen when you come home for Christmas.

I'm afraid to tell you that I haven't managed to get [30](through/off/hold/rid) of that book you needed for your course. However, I'm going up to London the week after next and I should be able to get it there. If you [31](went/played/wanting/fancied), we could meet up there and have lunch together. On the other hand, I know how much work you have to [32](go/put/pull/get) through and maybe you haven't the time.

Before I go, I must just tell you about a row which Mum and Dad had last week. It was ³³(making/taking/going/getting) *on* ³⁴(to/for/with/at) *seven o'clock and, out of the blue, Dad said he could* ³⁵(kill/die/murder/destroy) *a hamburger. I was* ³⁶(scared/dreading/worried/afraid) *Mum's reply because she had told dad earlier that we were having fish for supper and he clearly hadn't* ³⁷(mentioned/listened/taken/absorbed) *a word* ³⁸(of/up/in/on). *Mum hit the roof and looked at me, as if to say, "Don't* ³⁹(speak/stick/make/do) *up for your father. I know you are always* ⁴⁰(prejudiced/ picking/biased/turning) *against me in these situations."*

Unfortunately, this time she was correct. As you know, I'm not a great fan of fish but Mum's hamburgers are simply the best. Dad said "I'm sorry, darling, but I don't ⁴¹(fancy/like/wish/eat) *fish tonight, and anyway, I thought you said you wanted to get* ⁴²(through/by/to/over) *all the meat in the freezer before Christmas." Mum then shouted "If you want hamburgers, cook them yourself! I'm off." She slammed the front door in Dad's face as he followed her.*

Without speaking to him, I could already see that he regretted bringing up the subject of hamburgers. I suggested that we tried to ⁴³(take/get/let/make) *hold of one of those take-away pizza places but Dad said that he now felt a little under the* ⁴⁴(rain/fog/weather/snow) *and wasn't in the mood for food any longer. I thought how childish our parents had both been. It's occasions like this that put me off marriage.*

Lastly, I just wanted to say that during the Christmas holidays some friends and I are planning to go to the Natural History Museum to see the Dinosaur Exhibition. Would you like to come ⁴⁵(up/round/over/along) *too? You'd be most welcome. I'm really looking forward to seeing you when you break up from college.*

I love you, big sister!

Love

Craig   XXXXX

Lesson One

To come up

i. (To arise, to occur – usually unexpectedly)

Examples:
- Boss to secretary:
  *I'm off to lunch. If anything **comes up**,*
  you can get hold of me on my mobile (phone).
- *Phrasal verbs are bound to **come up** in this year's Proficiency exam.*

To come up, in this sense, usually suggests a problem which needs to be dealt with or something else abstract rather than physical (i.e. one **cannot** say *an accident came up*).
Also note that To crop up can be used in exactly the same way,
  e.g. *I'm dreadfully sorry but I won't be able to make it; something has just **cropped up**.*

ii. (To be mentioned, discussed)

Examples:
- *Did anything interesting **come up** at the meeting this morning?*
  It seemed to go on for ages.
- *Funnily enough, his name **came up** when we were*
  trying to work out who was involved with the take-over.

iii. (To approach in time, happening soon)

Examples:
- *We'll have to put off the trip to Paris until after Christmas*
  *because we've got quite a few important weddings **coming up**.*
- *The Managing Director's retirement must be **coming up**.*
  Who do you think is going to take over?

To come up with

i. (To think of a new idea)

Examples:
- *I've completely run out of ideas. Can you **come up with** something?*
- *I dread to think what the outcome will be*
  *if she doesn't **come up with** any answers.*

One should also note the expression To come out with which means to say something often unexpectedly or without any thought.
  e.g. 1. *My four year old son **comes out with** some very odd expressions from time to time.*
       2. *Please don't show me up by **coming out with** your usual nonsense.*

ii. (To be able to find the money to pay/to provide the money for something when it is needed or after it has been promised)

Examples:
- *They assured us that they would put up half of the capital but, when it came down to it, they didn't* **come up with** *the money.*
- *You've got to get it through to him that he must* **come up with** *a hundred thousand pounds by the end of the month, or face bankruptcy.*

To come up against (to come face to face* with problems – usually ones which are not expected)

Examples:
- *We're bound to* **come up against** *a few difficulties but we'll work them out.*
- *Even though I'm getting on in life, experience hasn't taught me to predict what I'm likely to* **come up against***.*

* Note that To come face to face with a problem is different from To face a problem. The former expression means to meet a problem by chance and the latter is used when one knows a problem exists and is now trying to deal with it.

To cater, catering (To provide food/the provision of food for a function – e.g. wedding)

Examples:
- *I wouldn't be able to cope with* **catering** *for such a large group of people.*
- *I know that Mrs. Jones is doing the* **catering** *this evening, but isn't there anything to be getting on with now?**

* i.e. *Is there something light we could eat now before the main meal this evening?*

To cater for (To deal with the specific desires, needs of a particular group of people, to accommodate)

Examples:
- *Apart from the fact that the hotel was filthy, it didn't really* **cater for** *young children.*
- *The owners of the restaurant reluctantly put themselves out to* **cater for** *my elderly relatives.*

To cater to (To make something more accessible to people, often by lowering standards, being more commercial – e.g. music, politics etc.)

Examples:
- *I wasn't taken in by what the President came out with.*
  *He was just trying to **cater to** the masses.* *
- *He has remained a highly sought-after singer,*
  *although he has refused to **cater to** the tastes of teenagers.*

To cater *to* and To cater *for* can be used in a very similar way except that To cater *to* has more of a negative feel about it.

* i.e. the ordinary people of the country.

Easy-going (Easy to please, does not make a fuss, relaxed)

Examples:
- *If you're too **easy-going*** *with your staff, they'll take advantage of you.*
- *We're not bothered what we do this evening;*
  *we're all **easy-going** people.*

In more colloquial English, the expression Laid-back is often used to describe a person, attitude, atmosphere or type of music which is very relaxed or relaxing.

e.g.
1. *He's not cut out for such a hectic life; he's far too **laid-back**.*
2. *You can't afford to adopt that **laid-back** attitude if you want to get on in this company.*
3. *In my office people often get too carried away with their work. Mind you,*
    *the atmosphere is very **laid-back**.*

* i.e. if you are too relaxed, informal with your staff.

*"If you're too **easy-going** with your staff, they'll take advantage of you."*

117

To go along with (To agree, to consent to)

Examples:
- *In the end she **went along with*** *their plans,*
  as she didn't want to be the odd one out.
- *We are reluctant to **go along with** your proposals for the*
  new town centre because they don't appear to cater for the disabled.

* In this example, **To go along with** is very similar to **To come round to** (see Page 14). Remember, however, that **To come round to** can only be used after a certain period of disagreement. **To go along with**, on the other hand, does not have to be used in this way (see 2nd example). It can also be followed with a person,
e.g.   *I go along with <u>you</u> as far as handling the first problem is concerned but I'm at odds with your views on the rest.*

It's just as well/it's a good job/it's a good thing (To be pleased that, "it's lucky that")

Examples:
- ***It's just as well*** *she didn't turn up at the opera,*
  because all the tickets had sold out quite a while ago.
- ***It's a good job*** *you didn't tell the boss what she*
  had said, because he would have hit the roof.
- ***It's a good thing*** *you were here:*
  I couldn't have done it without your help.

These expressions are used when one wishes to say that it is lucky that something happened or did not happen, otherwise there would have been negative consequences.

Ruthless (Cruel, acting without pity and compassion towards one's enemies or inferiors)

Examples:
- *I don't think he's **ruthless** enough to get on in this hectic city.*
- *It may seem **ruthless**, but unless you can come up with*
  an alternative, we'll have to sack half the workforce.

To mess around/about

i.   (To do nothing in particular) **Colloquial**

Examples:
- A: *What have you been up to recently?*
  B: *Oh nothing much, just **messing around**.*
- *I fancy spending this weekend just **messing about** at home.*

ii. (To interfere/play with something – especially a machine) **Colloquial**

Examples:
- *Please stop **messing around** with my camera; I know how clumsy you are.*
- *Do you want to come along or are you going to be here all day **messing about** with your car?*

iii. (To misbehave, mix with the wrong people, to have an affair with someone) **Colloquial**

Examples:
- *Teacher to student:*
  *Will you stop **messing around** and get on with some work!*
- *Mother to child:*
  *I don't want you to **mess around** with those nasty boys any more.*
- *I'm sure he's up to something;*
  *he's probably **messing about** with his secretary.*

iv. (To cause inconvenience by unreliability or by changing one's mind)

Examples:
- *I think I am going to hand in my notice soon.*
  *My firm have been **messing** me **around*** for too long.*
- *Look, stop **messing** me **about**!* Are you coming over tonight or not?*

Note also the colloquial expression To mess up which means to ruin, fail badly,
e.g.   1.   *She never takes in a word I say; I'm so afraid that she's going to **mess up** her life.*
       2.   *You can't afford to **mess** your exams **up** again this year.*

* There is a great difference between **To mess around/ about** *with* someone (See iii. above, Third Example) and **To mess someone around/about** as in these examples.

Let alone (Not to mention; and much less)

Examples:
- *He can hardly get by in his own language properly, **let alone** English.*
- *We can't even afford to take on a cleaner, **let alone** a first class secretary.*
- *She doesn't call on her mother very often, **let alone** her aunt.*

This expression basically means that the person cannot or does not do things which one would expect him or her to do. Therefore, he cannot be relied upon to do something more difficult or more unusual. It is used after a negative construction such as *can't, doesn't, hardly* etc.

To feel/To be hard-done by (Unfairly treated or punished, brought up* without luxury)

Examples:
- *They feel **hard-done by** because the newspaper article was clearly biased against them.*
- *We were **hard-done by** as kids. We didn't even have radios, let alone televisions and videos.*

Note also the expression Hard to *come by* which means difficult to find, obtain,

e.g. 1. *Cheap flats in London are **hard to come by** because they are so highly sought-after.*
2. *If you get hold of that book, you'll be very lucky. It's very **hard to come by**.*

* See **To bring up** (Page 52).

To make the most/best of
To make do with
To do **Colloquial**

i. (To use/manage something as best as one can, even though it is not really suitable, to put up with*)

Examples:
- *I could do with a better television but I suppose I'll have to **make the most/best of/make do with** the one I've got for the time being.*
Or *(The one I've got will have **to do**...)*
- *Even though I felt hard-done by, earning such a low salary, I **made the most/best of it/made do with** it.*
Or *(It had **to do**.)*

Note that To do can mean to be good enough, sufficient.

e.g. A: *Is this the kind of light you're looking for?*
B: *Yes, **that'll do** nicely.*

* See Page 62.

ii. (To take advantage of* something while it lasts because it is only going to be for a short time)

Examples:
- *Instead of messing around at home, we might as well **make the most/best of** this lovely weather we've been having.*
- *I want to **make the most/best** of my last month in London because I probably won't be back for quite a while.*

Neither **To make do** nor **To do** can be used in this sense of **To make the most/best of**.
* See Page 48.

Lesson Two

To get off

    i.   (To descend from a plane, train, bus, bicycle etc.)

        Examples:
- *It's a good thing we're **getting off** at the next stop: I could murder a cold drink.*
- One child to another:
  *Can you **get off** my bike and let my sister have a go?*

    ii.   (To stop touching something/someone)

        Examples:
- Mother to her children:
  *It's just as well you **got off** Mr Brown's car before he caught you. You'd have really shown me up.*
- Woman to man:
  ***Get** (your hands) **off**! If you touch me again, I'll do more than just tell you off!*

This meaning of **To get off** is very often used when someone is being very possessive about their property. Note also the colloquial expression To get (someone) off one's back which means to stop (someone) putting pressure on someone, or simply to stop **hassling** them. It suggests that the offender has been doing this for quite a while,

    e.g.   *If you promise to get on with this project, I'll try to **get** the boss **off** your back.*

    iii.   (To remove something which is awkward*, stuck, etc.)

        Examples:
- *The chewing gum has now been trodden into the carpet; you'll never **get** it **off**!*
- *Can you have a go at **getting** this lid **off**? It's impossible!*

* See Page 35.

    iv.   (To start a journey, to leave)

        Example:
- *It's getting on for 11 o'clock. I must be (**getting**) **off**.*

Compare with **To be off to** (see Page 78).

v.   (To send a letter – usually done in a hurry)

Example:
* *No matter what comes up, you must **get** these letters **off** straightaway.*

Compare with **to go off** (see Page 4).

vi.   (To receive little or no punishment, to escape serious injury)

Examples:
* *John felt hard done by because he got a prison sentence whilst all the other directors **got off** with a fine.*
* *It was a serious accident; it's a wonder he **got off** with only a few cuts and bruises.*

Note that this meaning of **To get off** has more or less the same meaning as **To get away with** (see Page 77). The only difference is that **To get off** can be used on its own at the end of a sentence, whereas **To get away** with has to be followed by a noun or simply **it**,

e.g.   *Everyone was convinced they committed the crime. We can't work out how they **got off**/ got away with it.*

Also, **To get off** has a narrower usage in that it usually applies to criminal matters in a legal sense, whilst **To get away with** can be used more generally.

*"Can you **get off** my bike and let my sister have a go?"*
(see Page 121)

To get out

i.   (To descend from the inside of a car, lorry, etc.)

Example:
- *Would you mind if I **got out** of the car?*
  I'm feeling a little under the weather.

Note that **To get** *out* can be used instead of **To get** *off* when concerning the removal of a stain (see Page 121, **iii.**) or when *getting someone/something **out** of one's mind*.
To get off is generally used for larger vehicles of transport, e.g. planes, ships, etc. (see Page 121, **i.**). Compare the following two sentences:
1.   *Get **off** my car!* (See Page 121, **ii.**)
2.   *Get **out of** my car!* (See above)

ii.   (To leave a place – often by order or in a hurry)

Examples:
- *She hasn't even **got out** of bed yet, let alone got off to work.*
- ***Get out** of the kitchen! You're putting me off my cooking.*
- *Come on, let's **get out** of here. They're just trying to mess us around.*

iii.   (To publish – usually a report or statement – often in a hurry)

Example:
- *I think we'd be better off **getting** this report **out** as soon as possible, rather than putting it off until after the law changes.*

This use of **To get out** is very similar to **To put out** (see Page 60).

iv.   (To say something, despite having difficulty, either because the subject is complicated/sensitive or because the person cannot express themselves very well)

Examples:
- *I'd prefer you to be straightforward with me and **get** it **out**.**
- *As a writer, she's much sought-after but on television, she can't seem to **get** her words **out**.*

* Compare with **To get on with** (see Page 106).

v. (To reach public knowledge, to become known – news, information)

Examples:
- *News has just **got out** that the two men prosecuted for kidnapping Mr. Smith have got off.*
- *The plans we have come up with today must never be allowed to **get out**.*

vi. (To avoid doing a task or something that one does not want to do – usually by giving a poor excuse)

Examples:
- *She thinks I pick on her but she always tries to **get out** of doing her share of the work.*
- *I can't come round on Sunday because I've been invited to a wedding which I can't **get out** of.*

Note the difference between **To get out of (doing) something** and To get something out of (doing) something which means to benefit, gain intellectually, emotionally or spiritually from doing a particular thing,

e.g.
1. *If you're not the kind of person who is prepared to put herself out for people, you won't **get anything out** of being a nurse.*
2. *We will arrange all the facilities, services and everything else you need; in the end what you **get out of it** is up to you.*

One should also be aware of the expression To get something out of someone which means to obtain useful information from someone, usually by pressure,

e.g. *I wouldn't bother asking John: you won't **get anything** sensible **out of him**.*

vii. (To borrow a book from a library)

Example:
- *Why don't you **get out** some handy books on catering from the library?*

Slip-up, to slip up (A small mistake, to make a small mistake)

Examples:
- *We just can't afford to make any more **slip-ups**.*
- *If he **slips up** again, he could mess up the whole deal for us.*

Outrageous (Ridiculous, unbelievable, very offensive, unreasonable)

Examples:
- *The Government has said that it will not cater to the **outrageous** demands of opposition MPs.*
- *I think it was an **outrageous** decision to call off the meeting, just because one person couldn't turn up.*

124

Note that Outraged means to be very angry, furious about something,
> e.g.   *He is generally such an easy-going character but*
> *he was **outraged** by the accusations they came out with.*

To come to terms with (To accept something negative, unpleasant or tragic which cannot be changed)

Examples:
- *After her accident, she didn't think she'd be able to cope but now she has **come to terms with** the fact that she will never walk again.*
- *It's at least three years since his wife went off with his best friend, but he still hasn't **come to terms with** it.**
- *We'll just have to **come to terms with** the recession and hope things pick up next year.*

* Compare with *he still hasn't **got over** it.*
(See Page 79.)

On the verge of (About to do something, likely to happen very soon)

Examples:
- *Although for many years the two countries were at odds with each other, they are now **on the verge of** signing the most important agreement in recent times.*
- *It looks like the company is **on the verge of** financial collapse; it could do with someone putting up a few million pounds.*

It is very common to hear this expression used with a nervous breakdown,
> e.g.   *It's a good job he gave up working: he was **on the verge of a nervous breakdown**.*

Also note the expression On the brink of which has more or less the same meaning but is slightly more formal,
> e.g.   *People are now coming to terms with the fact that we are **on the brink of** war.*

To crack up

i.   (To become mad, mentally ill, to have a nervous breakdown) **Colloquial**

Examples:
- *I can't cope with all the hassle I'm getting at work at the moment. I'm on the verge of **cracking up**.*
- *She takes on far too much work: She's bound to **crack up** under all this pressure.*
- *Monday morning: I could have sworn it was Sunday today. I must be **cracking up**!**

* This is a less serious use of **To crack up** than in the other examples. It simply means *I was sure it was Sunday. How silly of me!*

ii. (To laugh a lot, to make someone laugh) **Colloquial**

Examples:
- When he trod on the bank manager's foot,
  we all **cracked up** (laughing).
- If I'm feeling a little under the weather,
  I ask my cousin round. He always **cracks** me **up**.

There are many colloquial ways of saying **To laugh a lot**. Here is a list of some of them:

I laughed my head off when I saw her trip over the man's umbrella.
I creased up (laughing)...
I split my sides (laughing)...
I died laughing...
I was in hysterics...
I was in stitches...

Note also the expression It's not what/all/everything it's cracked up to be which means overrated, not as good as everyone says,

e.g. 1. *I don't know why you're raving about that film. It's not half of what it's **cracked up to be**.*
      2. *As a business man, he is somewhat underrated but*
          *as a lawyer, he is not all he is **cracked up to be**.*

To grasp (To succeed in understanding something – usually something complicated)

Examples:
- Sorry, I couldn't quite **grasp** what you were saying.
  Would you mind going over it again?
- I appreciate that this concept is difficult
  to **grasp**, but you'll soon pick it up.

To grasp literally means to hold something/someone tightly,

e.g. *It's just as well I **grasped** your arm when I tripped; otherwise I'd have hurt myself.*

A crackdown, to crack down on (Severe action taken by an official organisation against wrongdoers; to take severe action against people who break the law, rules, etc. or against what they do – e.g. tax dodging, terrorism etc.)

Examples:
- I'd now like to turn to the committee's plan of a
  crackdown on drug taking during the next Olympics.
- Did you read in the papers this morning that the
  Government is **cracking down on** tax-dodgers/tax dodging?
- The police have been put under pressure to come up with
  some new methods of **cracking down on** terrorism/terrorists.

Also note To clamp down on which has the same meaning but is perhaps a little less severe.

To reckon

i. (To think, estimate) **Colloquial**

Examples:
- *I don't **reckon** they'll take her on as a waitress; she's far too clumsy.*
- *How much do you **reckon** the installation of the new computer system will work out at?*
- *She **reckons** there'll be a very large turnout at the shareholders' meeting today.*

ii. (To be supposed/considered to be)

Examples:
- *Apparently, she's **reckoned to be** the brightest pupil this school has ever turned out.*
- *From what I can gather, it's **reckoned to be** the best car on the market.*

Lesson Three

To talk into (To succeed in persuading someone/oneself to do something)

Examples:
- *I knew he'd come round to it eventually.*
  *Who was it who **talked** him **into** changing his mind?*
- *I was reluctant to hand in my notice but*
  *in the end, I **talked** myself **into** it.*

The opposite of **To talk** *into* is To talk *out of*, i.e. to persuade someone *not* to do something,
> e.g. 1. *He was on the verge of jumping from the top floor, but the police **talked** him **out of** it.*
> 2. *She'll have to **talk** herself **out of** her depression. She doesn't have anyone else to turn to.*

To soak, get soaked (To put in water, to get very wet)

Examples:
- *You'd be better off **soaking** that jumper in*
  cold water than putting it in a hot wash.
- *It's just as well I brought my umbrella with me,*
  *otherwise I would have got **soaked**.**

* Instead of using **soaked** one can also use the word drenched.

To go through

i. (To experience a bad time, to suffer)

Examples:
- *They **went through** an awful time last year when*
  the Home Office started to crack down on illegal immigrants.
- *He must be **going through** hell,**
  now that his marriage is breaking up.

Note that in the Present Perfect form one can also use **have** *been* **through** instead of **have** *gone* **through**,
> e.g. *She's really **been** through it this year.*

The **it** refers to the bad period she has experienced.
* i.e. *having a terrible time.*

ii. (To complete, to last a period of time – i.e. a person)

Examples:
- *Even though I can get by in English,*
  *it takes me ages to **go through** a newspaper.*
- Wife to husband:
  *I'm very proud of you. You **went through** the*
  entire evening without dropping off once.
- *I've **gone through** almost a year having to*
  put up with this kind of hassle, so I'm quite used to it.

To go through and To get through (see Page 95) can be used in more or less the same way for this meaning. However, To *go* through is usually preferred when one wants to express the idea of something being completed quickly,
> e.g. *I **went through** the book in just half an hour.*

To *get* through, on the other hand, generally suggests that something has been difficult to finish,
> e.g. *It took me ages to **get through** that book.*

Another difference is that one can use To **get** through with a period of time without further information,
> e.g. *I don't know how I **got through** last week.* (See Page 95.)

One could *not* say, on the other hand, *I don't know how I **went through** last week*, unless some more information was added such as *...without seeing you.*

iii. (To go over, run over)*

Examples:
- *There's no point (in) trying to get out of **going through** it again;*
  not everyone has grasped the schemes you have come up with.
- *I can't be bothered to **go through** the figures with you now.*
  I'll get back to you tomorrow.
- *We've already **been through** that.*
  Haven't you taken in anything that's been going on?

* See Page 12 and Page 83, respectively.

iv. (To look at, examine someone's belongings – when one is intending to steal something or be nosey, to organise one's things into "wanted" and "unwanted")

Examples:
- *It's difficult coming to terms with a burglary when*
  *you know someone has **been through** all your things.*
- *When you have a moment, can you **go through** all your*
  cupboards and drawers and see what clothes you need to turn out?

v. (To use up, get through)

Example:
- *You've run out of teabags again.*
  *You **go through** them so quickly, don't you?*

See Page 95.

vi. (To be completed, to come into operation – e.g. a contract, law, etc.)

Examples:
- *If this deal doesn't **go through**, we may be able*
  to talk him into accepting an alternative offer.
- *He must be cracking up if he thinks that Parliament*
  *will allow an outrageous law like that to **go through**.* *

* Note that for this example *only*, **To get through** could also have been used (see Page 95), i.e. to be approved.

To go through with (To make a decision to complete or do something unpleasant or difficult after having doubts about doing it)

Examples:
- *For a while, they were getting on better but then they started rowing*
  *again, so in the end, my sister decided to **go through with** her divorce.*
- *Doctor to patient:*
  Mr. Smith, I have to warn you that the operation could leave you
  *paralysed. It's up to you if you want to **go through with** it.*

To scrap (To get rid of, to abandon an idea, system or law)

Examples:
- *We **scrapped** the old timetable because it wasn't working out.*
- *The British people are awaiting the outcome of recent*
  negotiations but are still hoping that the Government
  *will **scrap** the idea of joining the Euro.*

To lay off

i. (To make redundant)

Examples:
- *They won't call off the strike,*
  *unless we promise not to **lay off** any more workers.*
- *If we go through another year like this one,*
  *we'll have to **lay off** the majority of staff.*

Note the noun lay-offs, i.e. redundancies,

e.g.   *The Unions have said they will not stand for further **lay-offs**.*

ii.   (To stop giving someone a hard time, to leave someone alone/in peace, to cut out* – e.g. a bad habit, something unpleasant) **Slang**

Examples:
- *You've been having too much of a go at him recently.*
  ***Lay off** him for a while!°*
- *Wife to husband:*
  I won't get off your back until you lay off the booze.†

* See Page 59.
° i.e. *Leave him alone!*
† Booze is British slang for alcohol.

I might have known ("I should have guessed because it always happens; It's typical. It doesn't surprise me.")

Examples:
- ***I might have known** you would turn up late.*
- A: *He got out of doing the washing-up again.*
  B: ***I might have known**!*

To cringe (To show visibly that one is embarrassed – often because of what someone else does or says, "To die" of embarrassment)

Examples:
- *I'm so sure he's going to show me up in front of my clients;*
  *I just **cringe** (with embarrassment) every time he opens his mouth.*
- *I **cringe** at the thought of asking my uncle to*
  put up even more money than he has already lent us.

To see out/through

i.   (To complete something difficult, unpleasant or unsatisfactory, which has already been started)

Examples:
- *My business course is not what it's cracked up to be but,*
  *as there is only one month to go, I may as well **see** it **out/through**.*
- *To get on as a lawyer, you must have*
  *the determination to **see** things **through/out**.*

Students should now compare the following four expressions all relating to the idea of **completing** something:

1.   **To get through** (To manage to complete a difficult period of time, see Page 95.)
2.   **To go through** (To complete, last a period of time, see Page 128.)
3.   **To go through with** (To make a decision to complete something after having doubts, see Page 130.)
4.   **To see through** (above)

ii.   (To realise that someone is trying to deceive you)

Examples:

- *You can try and talk them into doing it your dishonest way, but they are bound to **see through** it in the end.*
- *There's no point (in) trying it on with me; I can **see through** exactly what you're up to.*

Note that only **To see** *through* and not **To see** *out* can be used to express this meaning.

iii.   (To be sufficient to last a specific period of time – usually money or food)

Examples:

- *We'll have to make do with the food I bought yesterday and anyway, it's probably enough to **see** us **through** the weekend/ to **see** the weekend **through/out**.**
- *Owing to the legal hassle we had with the landlords, we've only got £500 in the Company Account to **see** us **through** the rest of the year/ to **see** the rest of the year **through/out**.**

* Note that one *cannot* use the direct object pronoun (me, you, etc.) before **out** for this meaning, i.e. one *cannot* say *To see **us** out the weekend* but only *To see the weekend **out***.
Also note that **To get** *through* (see Page 95) could also be used instead of *To see us through the weekend* but one *cannot* say *To get the weekend through*.

iv.   (To accompany someone to one's front door in order to say goodbye to them, to let oneself out of someone's house, office without that person's help – i.e. "to see *someone* out")

Examples:

- *I'm just going to **see** Mr. Smith **out**.** *If anything comes up, I'll be back in a second.*
- *I must be getting off. Don't worry; I can **see** myself **out**,** thank you very much.*

Compare with To see off which means to say goodbye to someone who is going on a long journey, usually from an airport, station or port,

      e.g.   *We should all put ourselves out and go to the airport to **see** John **off**. He won't be back for quite a while.*

* Note that **To see through** *cannot* be used for this meaning.

To sink in (To be accepted as reality and therefore not just a dream/nightmare; to take what someone has said seriously)

Examples:
- Sports commentator to tennis star:
  *You're the youngest player ever to get through to a Wimbledon final. Has it **sunk in** yet?*
- *You'll only begin to get over the tragedy after everything has **sunk in**.*
- Mother to child:
  *What I said to you the other day just hasn't **sunk in**,* has it? What do I have to do to get my message across to you?*

* i.e. *You haven't **taken in** what I said to you the other day.* See Page 104.

Tacky (Something which looks very cheap and is full of bad taste) **Colloquial**

Examples:
- *Surely, it's not necessary for a company as well-off as this one to do up its offices in such a **tacky** way.*
- *I'm not bothered where we go to eat, as long as it's not one of those **tacky** fast-food places.*

*"You're the youngest player ever to get through to a Wimbledon final. Has it **sunk in** yet?"*

POLICEMAN AND VICTIM OF BURGLARY:

POLICEMAN: *Hello, Madam, may I come in? I've come round to investigate the burglary that was reported last night.*

WOMAN: *Oh, thank you, Officer. Actually I was on the verge of going out, but please come in. Sorry the place is in a state, but the burglars have been through everything. They've messed up the whole house – I don't think I'm ever going to come to terms with this.*

POLICEMAN: *Well, it'll probably take quite a while to sink in. Many people don't realise what it's like to go through a burglary.*

WOMAN: *I can understand the point of taking valuable items, but what do they get out of vandalism?*

POLICEMAN: *It's very hard to say, Madam. When we do catch people like this, it's very difficult to get anything out of them.*

WOMAN: *What are the odds on you catching these ones?*

POLICEMAN: *It depends on what we've got to go on. If they made a few slip-ups and left some clues, our chances are greater. But often, even if we catch them, they get off if there are no witnesses. What's actually missing?*

WOMAN: *Fortunately not that much; a few bits of tacky jewellery and the video. It's just as well I had most of my valuable jewellery with me. Also, it looks like they messed around with the television but, for some strange reason, they left it here.*

POLICEMAN: *Where were you for the evening?*

WOMAN: *Well, my husband and I run a catering business and we were out at a function. I reckon they must have watched us leave the house. Otherwise, they wouldn't have known there was nobody in. We always make a point of leaving some lights on, and the radio as well. When we got home, we were actually drenched because of the pouring rain. The last thing we expected was to come up against something like this. I honestly feel as though I'm going to crack up.*

POLICEMAN: *Please try to calm down, Madam. Once you've seen through these first few days, you'll be fine. You just have to talk yourself out of it. No-one was hurt and very little was stolen.*

WOMAN: *I suppose I'm feeling a little hard done by but I'll get over it.*

POLICEMAN: *Well I'll be getting off now. Please call if you need any help.*

SHOP ASSISTANT AND CUSTOMER:

ASSISTANT: *Good morning, Mr Miller.*

MR MILLER: *Hello there, Jim.*

ASSISTANT: *What can I do for you, sir?*

MR MILLER: *Well, I've been putting off doing up the house and now I realise it's a task I can't get out of. I need to buy some extra large picture hooks.*

ASSISTANT: *Unfortunately, we've just run out of them.*

MR MILLER: *Is it possible for you to get hold of some for me?*

ASSISTANT: *Well, they're quite hard to come by these days. Is it not possible for you to make do with these medium-sized ones? I think the company I use is going to scrap the larger ones.*

MR MILLER: *If that's all there is, I'll have to make the most of them. Also, I could do with some stain remover. Yesterday we went to the airport to see my brother off to Germany. As I got out of the car, I dropped a small bottle of whisky I was carrying in my coat pocket. It went all over the front car seats. I'm not sure if I'll be able to get the stain off.*

ASSISTANT: *The best thing to use is hot water and salt. Most of the stuff on the market at the moment is not what it's cracked up to be. They don't even get rid of simple food stains, let alone those caused by alcohol.*

MR MILLER: *Oh really, Jim, you do crack me up! You are not supposed to talk me out of buying things.*

ASSISTANT: *Well, if I tried to trick you, you'd see through it. I'm much better off being honest with my customers. Anyway, you can buy some salt from me if you wish.*

MR MILLER: *Can't you come up with anything more advanced than salt and hot water?*

ASSISTANT: *It's not ordinary salt. It's a special kind which caters for awkward stains. One tin like this should see you through the year.*

MR MILLER: *Really? That's very handy. OK, I'll take one. I hope the instructions are easy to grasp. I'm really clumsy with these things. Anyway, thank you very much for your help. I'll see myself out. Goodbye.*

WIFE: *How was your day?*

HUSBAND: *I had quite a bit of hassle in the office today. Apparently, news has got out that the company are about to lay off about a quarter of the staff.*

WIFE: *So they are going to go through with it then? I thought that you and the other directors decided that it was all uncalled for.*

HUSBAND: *It's Simon. He has come up with some new ideas for reshaping the company.*

WIFE: *Oh, I might have known such a ruthless scheme would come from him.*

HUSBAND: *It's not a question of being ruthless; it's what is necessary. This time I go along with him. We have to cater for the modern client who doesn't need ten people handling his affairs.*

WIFE: *It's just as well Simon's retirement is coming up; otherwise he'd have to make himself redundant.*

HUSBAND: *Oh, stop going on about him. He's a lot more easy-going than you make out.*

WIFE: *Just to change the subject: Has your client, Mr James, come up with the money he owes the company?*

HUSBAND: *It's funny that you should mention that. It came up at a directors' meeting we had yesterday lunchtime. I went through all the details with the others and then we decided we should get off a fax to him straightaway. It was left for me to do and I just cringed when I read the fax back to myself. It's so embarrassing asking old clients to pay up when you know they haven't got the funds.*

WIFE: *Yes, but he's been messing you around for ages. It's about time you stopped taking such a laid-back attitude towards him.*

HUSBAND: *Do you think you could lay off having a go at me for just five minutes?*

WIFE: *Of course, darling, enjoy your dinner!*

136

Chapter Six: Exercise

CHOOSE THE CORRECT WORD FROM THOSE IN BLUE
Answers on page 205.

GROUP DISCUSSION WITH TEACHER AND CLASS OF TEENAGERS:

TEACHER: *The first thing I'd like to discuss is the Togan Royal Family. What do you think of the behaviour of Prince Pietro and Princess Marta? Let's see if you can come [1](out/off/up/down) with some interesting points. Geoffrey, what are your thoughts?*

GEOFFREY: *Well, it's clear that Princess Marta feels hard [2](come/done/taken/given) by but in some ways, she only has herself to blame. I know she has been [3](through/along/down/across) a hard time, especially with the press, but she has to come to [4](cope/terms/accept/agreement) with the fact that the Togan public are interested in her life. Even though she tries to give the impression that no-one will get any information [5](out/from/away/beside) of her, it's easy to [6](see/go/be/come) through what she's up to. She wants everyone to know that she was on the [7](edge/risk/verge/side) of a nervous breakdown and that this was caused by her husband messing [8](up/around/over/together) with another woman.*

JILL: *I go [9](out/about/off/along) with Geoff to some extent. However, you have to remember that no-one had to [10](talk/encourage/force/persuade) Pietro into marrying Marta. If he loved someone else he should have married that person.*

TEACHER: *There has been talk of divorce. Do you think either of them really wants to go [11](finished/up/through/along) with it?*

TOM: *I think it's [12](upsetting/pity/unusual/outrageous) to force people to stay together if they are no longer in love. It is difficult to see what Pietro and Marta would [13](use/get/become/enjoy) out of remaining married. Eventually, either or both of them would [14](break/stick/crack/blow) up.*

JANE: *Well I must say, I don't [15](reckon/guess/estimate/belief) being a member of the Royal Family is all it's [16](made/taken/cracked/picked) up to be, if they have no private life and they have to attend boring events which they can't get [17](rid/out/avoid/free) of.*

TEACHER: *Well, it's [18](only/just/good/nearly) as [19](better/lucky/well/good) you weren't born into royalty. What does the class feel about royalty in general? Do we need a royal family on this island?*

PETER: *In my opinion, the Royal Family ought to be* [20]*(scrapped/divorced/executed/changed). There are thousands of people who are* [21]*(pulled/laid/take/pushed) off from their workplace every year. The money spent on the Royal Family should go to help the unemployed.*

JULIA: *It's easy to say we should get rid of the Royal Family. But what would we have instead? Some* [22]*(popular/funny/ruthless/clever) dictator probably. Other countries seem to have gone* [23]*(off/through/about/on) centuries without the monarchy but they can scarcely be said to be more democratic than us. Besides, they attract many tourists.*

PETER: *I* [24]*(might/will/ought/wish) have* [25]*(gathered/known/guess/believe) you would be a royalist! But I feel that when jobs are so hard to* [26]*(get/find/done/come) by, the Government shouldn't waste money on people who serve no useful purpose.*

TEACHER: *Well, that's all we have time for today. Let's pick up where we left off tomorrow.*

TWO OLD LADIES MEET ON A BUS:

PAT: *Hello, June. Fancy seeing you here!*

JUNE: *Patricia! What a nice surprise. What have you been up to these days?*

PAT: *Nothing very much; just* [27]*(taking/asking/messing/going) around at home with my grandchildren, who have come to stay with me over the summer holidays.*

JUNE: *Oh, how lucky you are. I rarely get to see my grandchildren these days...*

PAT: *Sorry to interrupt you, but can you tell me where to get* [28]*(off/on/out/away) for the Post Office.*

JUNE: *Yes, I'm going that way myself. Anyway, as I was saying, my eldest grandson is studying very hard. He was thinking of leaving college at one time, but his mother* [29]*(encouraged/talked/got/threw) him out of it. Now he has admitted that he would be better off* [30]*(sticking/seeing/keeping/making) his course through. My granddaughter has been waiting for an operation on her leg but the hospital keep* [31]*(messing/taking/bothering/disturbing) her around.*

PAT: *What happened?*

JUNE: *Apparently, she was* [32]*(hopping/getting/running/walking) out of the car when another vehicle came the other way and squashed the car door against her leg. She was lucky to get* [33]*(on/out/of/off) with the minor injuries she received. It could have been a lot worse. The other driver apologised and said he would compensate her for any expenses, but we doubt that he will come* [34]*(over/along/out/up) with the money. Anyway, how are your kids?*

PAT: *Well, unfortunately, they are not kids any more. James has recently opened his own training school which* ³⁵*(deals/handles/caters/specialises) for business people wishing to improve their knowledge of computers. John is making the* ³⁶*(worst/better/happiest/most) of his time left in Hong Kong. He is due to return at the end of the month. It seems like it was only a few months ago that we went to see him* ³⁷*(off/out/through/over) at the airport. Tracey is the easy-going one of the family. She's happy whatever she's doing and at the moment a few interesting contracts at work have* ³⁸*(appeared/come/arrived/turned) up. It's her children that are staying with me now.*

JUNE: *They must keep you busy. Have they brought with them plenty of video games and other things to do?*

PAT: *I don't even have a TV, let* ³⁹*(off/alone/along/out) a video. Oh no, they're quite happy messing* ⁴⁰*(together/out/up/around) with my husband's train set. Oh dear, I think I've just sat on a piece of chewing gum. I'll never get it* ⁴¹*(out/up/from/off) my coat.*

JUNE: *Oh Patricia, we have to get off here.* ⁴²*(Grasp/Pull/Push/Squeeze) my arm if you need support.*

Lesson One

To take to

i. (To like someone after knowing them for a short time, to like the idea of something, to be good at something almost immediately)

Examples:
- *I might have known those two idiots would **take to** each other; they've so much in common.**
- *The staff didn't **take to** the idea of us scrapping the old profit-sharing scheme.*
- *As you're so good at tennis, you're bound to **take to** squash.*

* Note that in relation to people, the expression To hit it off can also be used,
   e.g. *I can't work out why they didn't **hit it off**; they both come over as easy-going people.*

ii. (To start a bad habit)

Examples:
- *She'll never come to terms with the fact that her son has **taken to*** drugs.*
- *Her parents have been on the verge of cracking up since she's **taken to** staying out all night.*

* Compare with **To turn to** (see Page 86).

To get the hang of/To get to grips with (To understand how to use something/how something works or to understand a particular situation)

Examples:
- *I could do with some help; I can't **get the hang of** this computer at all.*
- *If you can get by in Spanish, it won't take you long to **get to grips with** Italian.*
- *The police have started looking into it, but it will take them quite a while to **get to grips with** the facts.*

To get the hang of is generally *not* used for a situation (e.g. the third example). It is usually employed in relation to how something works and therefore could also be used in the second example.
Also note the following two expressions, using the word **Grip**;

1. To get a grip on oneself/things which means to pull oneself together or take control of the situation,
   e.g. *Instead of feeling hard-done by, you'd better **get a grip on yourself/things** and start being a little more ruthless.*
2. To lose one's grip which means to lose one's power or control, ability or confidence,
   e.g. *I used to be so on the ball, but these days I feel **I'm losing my grip (on** everything).*

To spot (To notice something/someone which/whom is difficult to see)

Examples:
- TV advertisement:
  *Madam, I bet you can't **spot** the difference between these two washing powders.*
- *Having gone through the contract five times, I've **spotted** more than a few slip-ups.*
- A: *Can you **spot** Tom in the crowd? He's the one wearing that outrageous hat.*
- B: *Oh yes, I can just about make him out.*

Note the expression Spot-on which means exactly right,
e.g. *Yes, you're **spot-on**! Now I can see you're getting the hang of it.*

To put someone on the spot (To embarrass someone by asking them a difficult question)

Examples:
- *The interviewer tried to **put** the Prime Minister **on the spot**, but he managed to get out of giving a straightforward reply.*
- *She **put** her husband **on the spot** when, in front of his friends, she asked him what he had been up to the previous night.*

Compare with **To show up** (see Page 109) which means to embarrass someone in public by behaving in a certain way.
Note, to do something on the spot means to do something immediately, without hesitation,
e.g. *I wouldn't have stood for that sort of behaviour. Why didn't you sack him **on the spot**?*
Also note the expression To have a soft spot for which means to have affection for/to be fond of,
e.g. 1. *He always gets away with murder, but I must own up to **having** quite **a soft spot for** him.*
2. *I wouldn't rave about this part of England; mind you, I've got **a soft spot for** Cambridge.*

To be in a rut (To be stuck in a certain position in life or job, without the prospect of progress)

Examples:
- *I dread to think what my health will be like in ten years' time if I stay in this job; I'm already **in a** terrible **rut**!*
- *It's no good saying that you've just enough money to see you through the year: you have to get yourself out of this **rut**.*

To run down

i.   (To hit a pedestrian with a motor vehicle)*

Example:
- *I didn't spot that little man crossing the road. I nearly **ran** him **down**.*

One could also use **To run over** in the same way except that **To run down** is not usually used for small animals (see Page 83).

ii.   (To criticise, say bad things about someone/something)

Examples:
- *Not only is she stuck-up but she's always **running down** the other people in the office.*
- *It is not our purpose to **run down** the neighbouring schools, but they are simply too tacky for this posh area.*
- *Get a grip on things and stop **running** yourself* down. You'll never get through your exams with that attitude.*

* Note that when used in the reflexive form, it means to have a low opinion of oneself.

iii.   (To give someone a lift in a car)

Example:
- *I hope it's not putting you out, but would you mind **running** me (**down**) to the station?*

*"Get a grip on things and stop **running** yourself down. You'll never get through your exams with that attitude."*

iv.   (To bring to an end gradually, to decline)

    Examples:
    - *It is quite apparent that we can get by with a smaller army; therefore, many military divisions are going to be **run down** in the coming years.*
    - *From time to time the odd job will come up, but the Government do intend **running down** this particular department.*

This is usually used when referring to a government or some other official body which is reducing the funds available to a particular industry or operation.

To be/get run-down (To become exhausted, depressed over a period of time – often because of work, to get into a bad condition, to become neglected – a house, town, etc.)

    Examples:
    - *I could really do with a holiday; I'm so **run-down** at the moment.*
    - *I used to have a soft spot for this town but I went off it when it became so **run-down**.*

(A) run-down (A brief summary, report)

    Examples:
    - *I'll get back to you later and give you a **run-down** on what's likely to crop up.*
    - *Before things get too hectic, could you give me a **run-down** on the people who make up the Board of Directors?*

To run up (To accumulate costs – e.g. bills, debts, etc.)

    Examples:
    - *Waiter in a bar: Sir, do you wish to pay as you go along* or would you prefer to **run up** a bill?*
    - *I don't know if the business can handle any more expenses. We've already **run up** massive debts this year.*

Note that To run up against has the same meaning as **To come up against** (see Page 116).
* i.e. *each time you order something.*

(The) run-up (The period immediately before/leading up to something important and fixed in time)

    Examples:
    - *The Government are reluctant to take up the issue of party expenditure during the **run-up** to the elections.*
    - *He was completely unheard of prior to the **run-up** to the Olympics.*

This should not be confused with Runner-up, who is the person who comes second in a competition, election, etc.,

      e.g.   *I don't fancy his chances of winning; **runner-up**? ... Maybe!*

Guts (Courage to do something) **Colloquial**

Examples:
- *The problem with you is that you haven't got the **guts** to own up.*
- *Sticking up for yourself in front of the Board of Directors requires a lot of **guts**.*

To know what you are letting yourself in for (To be aware of the difficulties you will face, to know exactly what bad things are coming)

Examples:
- *I took it for granted that everything was going to be straightforward, but it turned out to be the other way round. I just didn't **know what I was letting myself in for** when I took on this project.*
- A: *I'm really looking forward to married life.*
- B: *I don't want to put you off, but you don't **know what you're letting yourself in for**!*

This expression is generally used in a *negative construction*, although even when used in a positive one, it still has a negative meaning (i.e. something bad happening),

      e.g.   *It serves him right; he **knew** perfectly well what he was letting himself in for.*

To undergo (To experience something inconvenient, unpleasant or difficult, to endure)

Examples:
- *In order to keep up with our competitors, our computer system will have to **undergo** a complete change.*
- *She may have to **undergo** surgery; it depends on the outcome of the tests.*

Clue (Something which helps one find an answer; evidence of a crime)

Examples:
- A: *You'll never guess what he came out with.*
- B: *Go on, give me a **clue**!*
- *The police are combing* the area for **clues**, but still haven't got much to go on.*

Note the informal expression I haven't got a clue which means **I've no idea**,

      e.g.   A: *Do you know where I can get hold of him?*
               B: *No, I'm sorry **I haven't got a clue**.*

* Combing in this sense means searching an area very thoroughly.

144

Lesson Two

Gimmick (An object which looks appealing but in fact serves no useful purpose, i.e. something which is for show only, words or promises designed to encourage people to believe or buy something)

> Examples:
> * *Apparently, the two retiring employees were outraged when they discovered that the watches they had been given by the company were merely* **gimmicks**.
> * *I'm not taken in by all this sales* **gimmick** *which shop assistants tend to come out with these days.*

Note the word Gimmicky (Colloquial) which means false, designed to attract attention only,
> e.g.
> 1. *Party Political Broadcasts are becoming more and more* **gimmicky**, *especially in the run-up to the elections.*
> 2. *I've had to come to terms with my husband's appalling taste in* **gimmicky** *ties.*

To come about (To happen, to take place)

> Examples:
> * A: *Business had been picking up but then, out of the blue, it dropped off again.*
>   B: *How did that* **come about**?
> * *I know you've been planning to take over the company for quite a while now, but when will it actually* **come about**?

To come about is often used after the interrogative pronouns **How?** and **When?** and generally in a way that expresses a degree of surprise or curiosity.

To make a meal of (To make something look more serious/difficult than it is)

> Examples:
> * *Maybe I'm biased but I think the players in your team* **make a meal of** *the injuries they receive.*
> * *Is he really in such a rut, or do you feel he's* **making a meal of** *it?*
> * *The lawyer* **made a meal of** *the contract. We would have been better off having a go at it ourselves.*

To pop/drop in (To pay a short visit) **Colloquial**

> Examples:
> * *As we're so near John's, we might as well* **pop**/**drop in*** *to see him.*
> * *Next time you run out of things to do, please* **pop**/**drop in** *to the office.*

Note To pop out (colloquial) which means to leave the office/house for a short while,

    e.g.   *I'm just **popping out** for a minute to drop Mr. Smith off at the station.*

Note also To pop down/along (colloquial) which means to go somewhere quickly and then come back,

    e.g.   *I only asked him to **pop down** to the shops and get me some milk, and he said I was picking on him!*

Thirdly, To pop up is a more colloquial way of saying **To come/crop up** (see Page 115),

    e.g.   *Sorry, I must be off; something's just **popped up** at the office.*

Also note To drop something in/round to someone, which means to take or return something to someone, usually when one is on one's way somewhere else,

    e.g.   *I'll **drop it in**/**round** (to you) this evening when I run my grandmother down to her club.*

* One could use **To pop in** but *not* **To drop in** if one spontaneously decides to go into a shop,

    e.g.   *I must **pop in** to the chemists to pick up some tablets for John. He's feeling a bit under the weather.*

Shove, to shove (A forceful push, to push with force)

    Examples:

-     *Give him a **shove**! I think he's dropping off.*
-     *In a shop queue:*
  *It doesn't matter how much you **shove**, I'm not going to let you push in.*

To fool (To trick, deceive someone)

    Examples:

-     *The local citizens won't take to being **fooled** by the council yet again.*
-     *Your lies will never **fool** me; I can see through everything you try on.*

Note the expression You could have fooled me! which means **It doesn't seem like it to me!**,

    e.g.   A: *Even though I failed my First Certificate, I'm an expert on getting through exams.*

           B: *Oh really?* **You could have fooled me!**

To slag off (To criticise strongly, to say very bad things about other people, a performance, etc.) **Slang**

    Examples:

-     *His film was **slagged off** by all the critics, but I think that it's underrated.**
-     *She makes out she has a soft spot for him but she's always **slagging** him **off** behind his back.*

* Note that when talking about the opinions of critics, as in this example, the verb To slate is often preferred.

To wind up

i. (To twist the screw on the side of a watch/clock or the handle of a car window in order to make it work/to close the window)

Examples:
- It must be quite a while since we last **wound*** the clock (**up**).
- Would you mind **winding up** the window? I'm getting soaked!

* Note the paradigm of **To wind** is **wind – wound – wound** and is pronounced like **bind – bound**.

ii. (To finish something, bring something to an end)

Examples:
- As we've got through practically everything we intended to discuss, we might as well **wind up** the meeting.
- I gather that the company is doing so dreadfully that the directors are thinking of **winding*** it **up** at the end of the year.

* Note that in English law, only a person can be made bankrupt and *not* a company. A company is either put into liquidation or is **wound up**.

iii. (To end up, to finish in a certain situation – often one which was not expected)

Examples:
- If you don't cut out smoking, you could **wind up** having to undergo heart surgery.
- After all that hassle, I was the one who **wound up** paying the bill they had run up.

iv. (To play a joke on someone, to fool* someone, "to pull someone's leg"°)
Colloquial

Examples:
- There's no need to hit the roof; I was only **winding** you **up**.
- I think he's making a meal of the whole issue. I'm sure she was just trying to **wind** him **up**.

* See Page 146.
° Note the expression To have someone on which has the same meaning,
  e.g.   I'm not that gullible! I know you're **having me on**.

v. (To become stressed, angry, to make someone angry)

Examples:
- *You shouldn't let yourself get so* **wound up** *at the office.*
  That's why you're so run down.
- *Don't get me wrong: I like your sister, but*
  she really knows how to **wind** *me* **up** *sometimes.*

To unwind/To wind down means to relax after being stressed,
  e.g. *After a hectic day in the office, I like to* **unwind**/**wind down** *by listening to some laid-back music.*
To wind down also has the same meaning as **To run down** in the sense of bringing to an end gradually (see Page 142),
  e.g. *I think we underrated the potential of our sports department.*
    We should never have **wound** *it* **down**.

To overshadow (To be made to look unimportant in comparison with something/someone else)

Examples:
- *He could never quite come to terms with the fact that his minor*
  achievements were **overshadowed*** *by his brother's great successes.*
- *The news that the company's turnover had almost doubled*
  was **overshadowed*** *by the sacking of the Managing Director.*

* This word is more often used in the passive voice.

To catch out

i. (To discover someone doing something which they should not be doing – often illegal)

Examples:
- *How did it come about that one of the directors was*
  caught (**out**) *giving secret information to a competitor?*
- *He thought that he would get away with it, but*
  eventually the tax inspectors **caught** *him* **out**.

ii. (To discover that someone does not know the answer to something that he/she ought to know – usually by asking them a difficult question)

Examples:
- *He's really on the ball. You'll never* **catch** *him* **out** *in a million years.*
- *I must own up to not knowing the answer.*
  You've **caught** *me* **out** *there; can't you give me a clue?*

Compare with **To put someone on the spot** (see Page 141).

148

L e s s o n   T h r e e

To bring about (To cause, make something happen)

Examples:
* The new evidence, which was previously so hard to come by,
  brought about the release of the prisoners.
* I'll go along with anything that has been proposed, providing
  that I'm convinced it'll ***bring about*** a breakthrough in negotiations.

To be/get (things/something) under way (To get started)

Examples:
* Introduction to a meeting:
  *Before we **get things** properly **under way**,*
  I'd like to bring up a few minor points.
* Football commentator:
  *The second half has just **got under way**, but*
  I'd like to pick up on what I was saying just before the break.

To plunge

i.   (To fall, go down suddenly/quickly)

Examples:
* *Today, share prices **plunged** to an all-time low;**
  a fact brought about by a lack of confidence in overseas trade.*
* *I don't really fancy crossing that bridge; last year it
  collapsed and quite a few cars **plunged** into the river.*

Note also the verb To plummet which can also be used in this sense of the verb **To plunge**.
* This is another way of saying *the lowest they have ever been.*

ii.   (To push an object into something/someone – usually a knife)

Example:
* A: *How did his death come about?*
  B: *Apparently, his wife **plunged** a knife straight into his heart.*

iii. (To get very interested, involved in a particular activity, subject)

Examples:
- *If you **plunge** yourself into your studies,*
  there's a chance you might get carried away.
- *Before we **plunge** ourselves into debate, could you give*
  me a run-down on what matters you'd like me to go over?

To take the plunge (To take a big risk in doing something which cannot be reversed at a later date – especially in business or marriage)

Examples:
- *If we don't **take the plunge** now, it'll serve*
  us right if our competitors beat us to it.*
- *At first, she didn't think she could go through with the marriage but,*
  *when it came down to it, she decided to **take the plunge**.*
  She doesn't know what she's letting herself in for!

* i.e. *...if our competitors get there first.*

I/I'll tell you what! ("I've got a good idea", "listen!") **Colloquial**

Examples:
- ***I tell you what**: why don't we catch you up later?*
- ***I'll tell you what**: they won't get away with it next time.*

To get into

i. (To get involved with, interested in something)

Examples:
- *It took me quite a while to **get into** this job but*
  now I've really got the hang of it.
- *I don't think I'll ever get through this book;*
  *I can't seem to **get into** it.*

Compare with **To plunge** (see Page 149). They are very similar in meaning but **To get into** is much more common in everyday usage.

ii. (To be accepted into a prestigious or competitive profession, college, etc.)

Examples:
- *Well-paid jobs in marketing are highly sought-after these days,*
  *which is why the profession is so difficult to **get into**.*
- *Have you heard about Jane? She's just **got into** Cambridge.*

Note the expression *What's got into you/him/her, etc?* which is used to ask why someone is behaving so strangely (See **To come over**, Page 12),

e.g.
1. *I'd love to know* **what's got into him** *lately. He really is an odd bloke!*
2. A: ***What** on earth* **has got into you**?
B: *I'm sorry, I don't know what came over me but I'm feeling rather run-down at the moment.*

On the off-chance (In the unlikely event)

Examples:
- *I asked him round* **on the off-chance** *he would accept my invitation but of course he turned it down.*
- A: *How come you knew I was in?**
B: *I didn't, I just came over* **on the off-chance**.

* i.e. *at home.*

To fall for (To be tricked, to believe a ridiculous story)

Examples:
- *I told him that I had been made Managing Director and, being so gullible, he* **fell for** *it.*
- *I thought she would* **fall for** *my little plan but, unfortunately, she saw through exactly what I was trying to do.*

Do not confuse **To *fall for* something** (See above) with **To *fool* someone** (see Page 146). **To fool** means to trick, while **To fall for** means to be tricked,

e.g. *I tried to* **fool** *him, but he didn't* **fall** *for it.*

*"It took me quite a while to **get into** this job but now I've really got the hang of it."*
(see Page 150)

To pull through (To survive a difficult time, a very dangerous operation, to recover from a very serious illness or to pass an exam)

Examples:
- *It would be wise to start considering alternative employment, on the off-chance the company doesn't **pull through** the recession.*
- *We were so relieved to hear that, having taken the decision to go through with the operation, she **pulled through** comfortably.**
- *She's not really up to taking the Proficiency exam. Mind you, she could just pull through.°*

* i.e. easily, without any problems.
° **To pull through** is very similar in meaning to **To get through** (see Page 95), except that the latter is not generally used for a hospital operation and **To get through** is more common as far as exams are concerned.

To call in

i. (To ask a professional or expert person/a group of people to come to help, to demand that someone enters a place for a particular purpose, to be summoned, e.g. to an office)

Examples:
- *The police were **called in*** to break up the fight.*
- *Please don't bring up the fact that I was **called in** to the boss's office this morning.*

* Compare with **To call on** (see Page 56) which is appealing for action usually from the public rather than a professional person or group of people.

ii. (To pop in*)

Example:
- *I'll try and **call in** on my way round to John's.*

* See Page 146.

iii. (To make a phone call to one's office/place of work – usually in order to explain where one is/why one is not there or to find out what has been happening in one's absence)

Example:
- *I'm feeling a little under the weather this morning. I think I'll **call in** and ask for the day off.*

Highly-strung (Very nervous, excitable, neurotic person)

Examples:
- *You must tread carefully with her. She is so **highly-strung** that she's likely to fly off the handle without warning.*
- *I think he may be a bit too **highly-strung** for this job; we need someone a little more laid-back.*

This expression is generally used to describe a person's general character, rather than how or she feels at a particular time or in relation to a specific incident; i.e. one would *not* say *I felt highly strung about my exams.*

"Maybe I'm biased but I think the players in your team
***make a meal of** the injuries they receive."*

(see Page 145)

INTERVIEW WITH MUSICIAN:

INTERVIEWER: *Before the interview gets under way, I'd like to give you a run down on what's likely to come up. I won't be trying to catch you out with tricky questions – otherwise we'll wind up having a row. I'd firstly like to concentrate on the earlier years of your career, before your music really caught on, and then, without putting you on the spot, I'd like to talk about your family life and future plans. Is that OK?*

MUSICIAN: *Fine.*

INTERVIEWER: *OK, then let's begin. You started as a drummer, but turned into a singer. How did that come about?*

MUSICIAN: *Well, I got myself into a rut playing drums. I needed to plunge myself into some other form of expression and so I had a go at singing. I was surprised but I really took to it, even though it took me a while to get to grips with all the scales. I started writing songs as well, which at first the other guys in the band couldn't get into. Then we called in the famous producer, Mike Smith, to see if he could spot where we were going wrong. He said our sound was too gimmicky and that our music needed to undergo a complete change of direction. We listened to him, even though at first we were slagged off by all the music critics; but then things started to work out.*

INTERVIEWER: *Are you saying that it was Mike Smith who brought about your new-found success?*

MUSICIAN: *In many ways, yes; but also you have to say that it was the members of the band who had the guts to take the plunge. We risked losing all our fans – but luckily it all turned out fine.*

INTERVIEWER: *As a travelling musician, I don't suppose you've had much time to spend with your family.*

MUSICIAN: *That's right. I didn't know what I was letting myself in for when I first started touring. It was great fun of course, but I didn't get the time to see my wife and kids. I used to feel that my success as a musician was overshadowed by my failure as a husband and father; but now I think I was unfairly running myself down. I've always had a soft spot for both of my daughters. Now they've grown up, we still have a lot of fun together. They're always winding me up about my old fashioned clothes. They say that I haven't got a clue on how to dress.*

INTERVIEWER: *And what of your plans for the future?*

MUSICIAN: *Who knows? Maybe I'll spend the rest of my days on a Pacific island, unwinding to the rhythms of the ocean...*

CONVERSATION BETWEEN FATHER AND DAUGHTER:

FATHER: *Where on earth did you get to last night?*

DAUGHTER: *Oh, I just popped into Sylvia's.*

FATHER: *Popped in? You could've fooled me. You must have spent half the night round there.*

DAUGHTER: *Well I didn't know if she would be in but I went round on the off chance. I wanted to congratulate her on getting into Cambridge.*

FATHER: *Sylvia? Cambridge? What's got into you? You must be winding me up of course.*

DAUGHTER: *No I'm not! I tell you what: she worked damn hard to pull through those exams. During the run up to the exams, she never went out once. You can't imagine how nervous she became. She's highly strung enough as it is......... Anyway, she's very happy. As a joke, she told her dad that Cambridge was too stuck-up for her and she preferred to go to Leeds.*

FATHER: *Did he fall for it?*

DAUGHTER: *Oh yes, he wondered what had come over her and told her to get a grip on herself. However, he soon realised she was having him on and they both laughed about it later.*

To change the subject; would you mind running me down to Peter's after dinner? Apparently, he got injured playing football last Sunday and can't go out.

FATHER: *Are you sure he's not just making a meal of it to attract your sympathy?*

DAUGHTER: *Oh, Dad! Of course not. He'd know I'd catch him out if he tried anything on like that.*

FATHER: *Very well, but don't come back late this time.*

155

Chapter Seven: **Exercise**

CHOOSE THE CORRECT WORD FROM THOSE IN BLUE
Answers on page 205.

A BOSS WELCOMING A NEW SECRETARY ON HER FIRST DAY AT WORK:

BOSS: *Hello there. I'm Trevor Bailey. You must be Tracy Lloyd.*

SECRETARY: *That's right.*

BOSS: *Please take a seat and make yourself comfortable. Well I must say, I hope you know what you are* [1]*(getting/taking/allowing/letting) yourself in* [2]*(for/to/at/by) coming to work here... Don't worry, I was only joking! I will give you a* [3]*(summary/run/show/brief) down on what you need to know. You will soon get the* [4]*(use/way/grips/hang) of things around here and, besides, everyone is really friendly and helpful.*

                  For the first few days you will probably feel that you haven't got a [5]*(idea/clue/opinion/evidence) about what's going on. I sometimes feel that way myself; especially since the company* [6]*(underwent/accepted/had/received) a complete change of personnel last year.*

SECRETARY: *What* [7]*(is/brought/took/was) that about?*

BOSS: *Well, it's a long story; but we nearly had to* [8]*(close/pull/wind/finish) up the company. The previous Managing Director* [9]*(caused/took/plunged/pulled) the company into massive debt and many members of staff had to be laid off.*

SECRETARY: *That's a great shame. Funnily enough, the same thing was on the verge of happening where I used to work. The Board of Directors had run* [10]*(up/out/through/off) debts they couldn't pay. Luckily they found a sponsor that helped them* [11]*(get/go/pull/push) through, and the company was saved.*

BOSS: *Why did you leave, then?*

SECRETARY: *Well, there were quite a number of reasons. Firstly my boss was extremely highly* [12]*(tempered/motivated/strung/educated). He would often get* [13]*(broken/messed/picked/wound) up by the easiest of problems and then he would make a* [14]*(mountain/business/meal/case) of issues which other people would ignore. He began to lose his* [15]*(control/strength/grip/way) and, although in some ways I had a soft* [16]*(centre/feeling/attraction/spot) for him, I couldn't cope with it any longer.*

SECRETARY: *Also, I had got myself into a* [17](*rut/boredom/routine/spot*) *and I noticed that everyone was running each other* [18](*through/down/over/up*). *I needed a change. I even thought of trying to get* [19](*to/out/off/into*) *university but then I thought that would really be taking the* [20](*plunge/jump/risk/action*). *Then I saw an advert for this job and thought I should give it a go.*

BOSS: *And I'm very glad you did. Well, let's get things* [21](*underway/beginning/starting/initiated*). *Your hours are 9.30 to 5.30 and I would appreciate it if you* [22](*popped/called/visited/ring*) *in by 9, if you're sick. I'm sure you'll take* [23](*in/up/to/from*) *the work. I will try to make it as interesting as possible for you... Please feel free to* [24](*pop/drop/come/take*) *out for a sandwich whenever you're hungry. Now, I'll just go and bring in your work and let you get* [25](*into/over/off/at*) *it.*

TWO BROTHERS GOING FOR A DRIVE:

ADRIAN: *Be careful! You nearly ran that old lady* [26](*up/down/through/across*).

PETER: *Don't worry, I've been driving for ten years.*

ADRIAN: *You could have* [27](*tricked/deceived/joked/fooled*) *me!*

PETER: *How come you're always slagging off my driving?*

ADRIAN: *I don't know what's* [28](*gone/come/got/taken*) *into you. I was only* [29](*making/getting/joking/winding*) *you up. I tell you what: why don't we call* [30](*up/out/in/of*) *on John? Apparently he's been feeling a little* [31](*run-through/special/run-down/run-over*) *recently. I'm sure he could do with cheering up.*

PETER: *Don't you remember the last time we turned up on the* [32](*hope/desire/thinking/off-chance*) *he would be in? We* [33](*brought/took/caught/got*) *his father out with another woman.*

ADRIAN: *Oh, of course! How could I forget. We really* [34](*dropped/made/put/pushed*) *him on the* [35](*spot/case/centre/go*) *– he was completely stuck for words. Do you remember, he kept trying to convince us that the woman was interested in buying those* [36](*jewellery/gimmicks/rubbish/tacky*) *he sells for a living? He didn't really expect us to* [37](*land/fall/go/run*) *for that did he? It was quite obvious what he was up to.*

PETER: *Well, I suppose we might as well go to the pub. It's the best way to* [38](*enjoy/unwind/wind/play*) *after a hard day's work.*

Chapter Eight
Lesson One

Patch

i.   (A piece of material used to cover holes in clothes or an injured eye)

Examples:
- *The teacher called him in to her office and told him*
  *off for wearing so many **patches** on his jeans.*
- A: *Why is that singer always wearing a **patch** (over his eye)?*
  B: *It's not for real; it's just a gimmick.*

ii.   (A small area, or part of something which is different from the rest –
e.g. in a building, on a body)

Examples:
- *Even though we've had the house done up,*
  *there are still quite a few damp **patches** on some of the walls.*
- *The first time I realised he was getting on*
  *was when I spotted a bald **patch** on the back of his head.*

iii.   (A difficult period of time)

Examples:
- *John thinks that she makes a meal of everything, but*
  *I honestly believe that she's going through a bad **patch** at the moment.*
- *If this bad **patch** goes on much longer,*
  we'll have to scrap all plans for a wage rise.

Note the expression Not a patch on, which means nowhere near as good as,
e.g.   *In France he's the most sought-after person in the game, but*
       *the Italians reckon he's **not a patch on** any of their players.*

Patchy

i.   (Good in some parts only)

Examples:
- *The film got rave-reviews, but I thought it was rather **patchy**.*
- *I wouldn't take what he says for granted;*
  *he's only got a **patchy** grasp of what's really going on.*

ii. (Appearing in irregular quantities and at various places – often used for the weather)

Examples:
- *There has been a serious hold-up on the main road leading out of Manchester because of* **patchy** *fog.*
- *You ought to make the best of the* **patchy** *spells of sunshine we're enjoying today; it's going to pour down* tomorrow.*

* i.e. rain heavily.

To patch up

i. (To repair – usually holes in clothes)

Example:
- *Your jacket could do with* **patching up**.

ii. (To make up*, settle an argument)

Example:
- *My partners haven't been getting on too well recently; I only hope that someone can talk them into* **patching** *everything** **up**.

* See Page 72.
Note that this meaning of **To make up** is intransitive (i.e. there is *no direct object*), whilst **To patch up** is transitive (i.e. there must be a direct object – in the example given, the object is *everything*).

"Your jacket could do with **patching up**.*"*

To turn on

i. (To switch on something electrical)

Example:
- *I nearly hit the roof when you **turned** the light **on** last night. Didn't you realise the children were fast asleep?**

* Note the opposite of fast asleep (sleeping deeply) is wide awake (completely awake).

ii. (To attract someone sexually, to excite) **Colloquial**

Example:
- *I find it really odd that you fancy him. He doesn't **turn** me **on** at all.*

Note the noun Turn-on:
e.g. *I used to find high heels a **turn-on**, but now they make me cringe.*
Also note the expression To turn someone on to something/someone which means to get someone interested in something/someone or to introduce something.
e.g. 1. *The thought of doing exercise used to be quite daunting, until one of my friends **turned me on to** cycling.*
2. *The only reason why I look up to my brother is because he **turned me on to** Woody Allen.*

iii. (To attack someone considered to be a friend or who is a member of the same family or on the same side in a war – physically or verbally)

Examples:
- *It was appallingly ruthless of the army to **turn on** its own people.*
- *I don't think **turning on** your mother like that was really called for.**

Be careful not to confuse **To turn *someone* on** (See ii. above) and **To turn *on* someone** (See above)!
* i.e. *necessary* (See **Uncalled-for** Page 107).

iv. (To depend on – used in respect of the result or success, depending on a particular thing)

Examples:
- *It'll all **turn*** **on** how well the judge gets to grips with the case.*
- *The outcome of the elections will **turn*** **on** which party can offer the most attractive gimmicks.*

* Note that for the purposes of intonation, *turn* should be stressed rather than *on*, as in meanings i. to iii. above.

To put down

i.   (To run down*, criticise, humiliate)

Example:

- *I didn't mean to **put** you **down** the other day;
  it was just the way it came over.*

* See Page 142.
Note also the noun Put-down which is a comment or statement that puts someone down or makes them feel stupid or useless,

e.g.   *Telling me that because I was getting on, I'd have to make do with a lower salary,
was a real **put-down**.*

ii.   (To write a word/words* – usually as a note or on a form)

Examples:

- *If you **put down** what I've just said,
  I won't have to go over it again tomorrow.*
- *When answering the question on the form about health,
  he **put down** that he had undergone psychotherapy.*

* Note one *cannot* say *To put down a letter, postcard, etc.*

iii.   (To crush, defeat by force, put an end to a rebellion, riot)

Examples:

- *The peasants put up a brave fight but were eventually
  put down by the Government's armed forces.*
- *The local police have got a lot to answer for
  over the way they **put down** this rather small riot.*

iv.   (To have a pet or other domestic animal killed by a vet* because
           it is very ill/old)

Example:

- *As it was unlikely that our dog would pull through the operation,
  we thought it would be kinder to have him **put down**.*

* Vet is an abbreviation for Veterinary Surgeon.

161

To put down to (to be explained by, to consider that something is caused by something else)

Examples:
- *He reckoned that his young looks could be* **put down to** *an easy-going lifestyle.*
- *We took the plunge, but unfortunately it didn't work out; let's just* **put it down** *to bad luck.*

Note the expression To put it down to experience which means that one should learn by what has happened and not be depressed by it,

e.g. *It hasn't sunk in yet, but I think you'd be better off* **putting it down to experience**, *rather than losing any sleep over it.*

This expression is quite different from **To put something down to** *lack of* experience which means that the failure or problem has been *caused by* one's lack of experience.

To put down for (To take a note of/to reserve a place in someone's name for a particular purpose)

Examples:
- *If you get hold of some tickets, can you* **put** *me* **down for** *two?*
- A: *Shall I* **put** *your wife* **down for** *the dinner at Christmas?*
- B: *Oh yes, she'd love to come along.*

To be/come/get up to scratch (To be/make something good enough, as good as it should be – often used in the negative)

Examples:
- *I can get by in Spanish, but my French* **is** *not quite* **up to scratch**.
- *The new ABC computer has a lot of amusing gimmicks but quite frankly, it doesn't* **come up to scratch**.
- *You'd better* **get** *your fitness* **up to scratch**, *if you want me to put you down for the local marathon.*

From scratch (From the beginning, from nothing)

Examples:
- *Why don't we just scrap the whole idea and start* **from scratch**?
- *I tell you what; it's going to be a hassle building it right* **from scratch**.

162

To come off

i. (To become separated from, unstuck after being attached to something, to be removable – e.g. a stain)

Examples:
- *No wonder the door handle **came off***; *you keep messing around with it.*
- *I was in stitches yesterday when she dropped the paint all over their carpet. It'll never **come off**.**

* Compare with **To get off** (see Page 121).
To get off is transitive,
       e.g.   *You'll never **get** that stain **off**.*
To come off is intransitive,
       e.g.   *That stain will never **come off**.*

ii. (To be successful, effective – usually a plan or idea)

Examples:
- *Don't take it for granted that the scheme will **come off**; we'll have to talk many people into going along with it.*
- *If it doesn't **come off** this time, she's bound to come up with something else.*

Compare with **To work out** (see Page 26).
To work out can be used in the examples above, but **To come off** is not generally employed for relationships (see examples of **To work out**).

iii. (To end up, to finish in a certain condition, situation after a difficult period of time, accident, investigation or some other incident)

Examples:
- *If the economy picks up, we could **come off** quite well* out of this take-over.*
- *After the accident, the passengers got off with a few cuts and bruises, whilst the driver **came off** the worst* with a broken neck.*
- *It was quite apparent that after the Government inquiry had looked into the conduct of various companies, they would **come off** rather badly.*

* This sense of **To come off** is often followed by *well/badly, best/worst*.

iv. (To stop taking medicine, alcohol, etc.)

Examples:
- Funnily enough, I got over the illness as soon as
I **came off** the antibiotics.
- Unless he **comes off*** the booze, he's going to mess up his life.

* Compare with **To lay off** (see Page 130).

To dither (To fail to reach a firm decision, to hesitate)

Examples:
- I wish you'd stop **dithering** and make up your mind.
- We can't afford to **dither**; either we take up
the offer or we allow the business to wind down.

Note also the expression To sit on the fence which describes a person, often a politician, who does not like to take sides or to make a firm commitment to a particular way of thinking, i.e. to be neutral. It is usually considered to be a criticism.

> e.g.   Minister, I'm sorry to put you on the spot, but wouldn't you agree that you have **sat on the fence** on many issues during the run-up to the elections?

Drawback (Disadvantage, defect)

Examples:
- I'm glad the boss came round to the idea of scrapping the old
computer system. The only **drawback** is that the new one
we have installed will work out to be far more expensive.
- The new secretary is on the ball and very efficient.
Her only **drawback** is that she's a bit bossy.
- I think the new photocopier is not a patch on the old one;
it has so many **drawbacks**.

Overheads (The expenses of running a business)

Examples:
- Providing that we cut down our **overheads**,
we should be able to get through the year.
- If we take on these premises, our **overheads** will go through the roof.

To take it out on (To be very unpleasant to someone for a reason which has got nothing to do with them or is not their fault – usually with a member of the same family, staff or a close friend)

> Examples:
> - Husband to wife:
>   *I'm sorry I had a go at you last night, but my work is really getting to me at the moment, and you're the only one I can **take it out on**.*
> - *Just because you're going through a bad patch, there's no need to **take it out on** the kids.*

To get one's own way (To get exactly what one wants – usually after a period of time)

> Examples:
> - *He may seem easy-going, but I tell you what: he always **gets his own way**.*
> - *He tries to take advantage of his mother's good nature, but I never let him **get his own way** (with me).*

Lesson Two

To fall out with (To stop being friends with someone after having had an argument with them)

Examples:

- He **fell out with** his partners **over** their decision to call in the tax inspectors.
- Let's make up! There's no point in **falling out** (**with** each other) over such a silly matter.

To take it/everything/something in one's stride (To deal with life's problems without making a fuss* and in a calm manner)

Examples:

- His sister is very highly-strung but he, on the other hand, **takes everything in his stride**.
- A year ago I couldn't cope with the hassles of the job but now, I **take it all in my stride**.
- She **takes** divorce **in her stride**; mind you, she's been through three of them!

A stride is the length of one's step when walking or running.
* See Page 3.

Off the top of one's head (Without needing to refer to information written down, without preparing beforehand)

Examples:

- If you can't remember the details **off the top of your head**,* get back to me on it later.
- A: Can you give me some hints on how to prepare a speech?
- B: Not really; I just do it **off the top of my head**.°

* Note that Off-hand could also be used for this example only. It also means to deal with someone in an unfriendly manner,

       e.g.   *She was very **off-hand** with some of the customers yesterday. I can't think what has come over her.*
° i.e. *I just improvise.*

To get round

i. (To avoid having to deal with a problem, law, rule, etc.)*

Examples:
- *We'll have to start from scratch, unless you can come up with a way of **getting round** the problem.**
- *The Government have said they will crack down on property developers trying to **get round** the Landlord and Tenant Act.*

Note that **around** is often preferred to **round** and can be used for all meanings.
* Compare with **To get over** (see Page 79).

ii. (To spread, circulate – news)

Examples:
- *The news soon **got round** that the Prime Minister had fallen out with the rest of the Cabinet.*
- *You should tell the boss what's going on before it **gets round** the office.*

iii. (To persuade someone to come round – usually for a specific purpose – i.e. "to get *someone* round") **Colloquial**

Examples:
- *I think we should stop messing about and **get** him **round** here straightaway.*
- *Why don't you **get** my uncle **round**? He'll get rid of those damp patches for you.*

Compare with **To ask someone round** (see Page 14), which is less forceful.

iv. (To get your own way with a person* who is in charge, e.g. parent or boss, often by paying them compliments, flattering them, i.e. "to get round *someone*"°) **Colloquial**

Examples:
- *You'll never persuade the boss to come round to our plans, if you adopt that aggressive attitude. Why don't you let me have a go at **getting round** him?*
- A: *I can't get over what a generous guy you are.*
  B: *Don't try and **get round** me; I know what you're up to!*

* See Page 165.
° Compare construction with **iii.** above.

v. (To be able to travel around)

Examples:
- *My grandmother is getting on for ninety but she still manages to **get round**.*
- *I'm probably going to take up driving again. I can't **get round** without a car.*

Note that To get about can also be used for this meaning.

To get round to (To find the time to do something – usually a task)

Examples:
- *I've been meaning to write to you for quite a while now but I just haven't **got round to** it.*
- *I must **get round to** doing up the house. What a hassle!*

To fork out (To pay for something or spend money reluctantly*) **Colloquial**

Examples:
- *He finally **forked out** the £20 he owed me, after messing me around for so long.*
- *The only drawback was that I had to **fork out** for the odd parking fine.*

Note the expression To shell out which has the same meaning.
Compare **To fork out** with To splash out, which means to spend money freely, usually on luxury items.
  e.g. *We've just **splashed out** on a new dishwasher, which I suppose we could have done without.*
* See Page 14.

*"He finally **forked out** the £20 he owed me, after messing me around for so long."*

168

It's nothing to write home about (Nothing special, ordinary)

Examples:
- *My sister raves about Australian wine, but*
  I think ***it's nothing to write home about***.
- A: *What was your holiday like?*
  B: *Well, the weather was a bit dodgy, and the hotel*
  was ***nothing to write home about*** *either.*

Also note the expression Run of the mill which has more or less the same meaning.

To make of

i.   (To think of, have an opinion about)

Examples:
- *The last accountant we took on was nothing to write*
  home about, but what do you ***make of*** *this new one?*
- *I wonder what his colleagues* ***made of***
  his decision to stand for Parliament.
- *I really don't know what to* ***make of*** *all these take-overs.*

Very often used in a question or after the verbs **To know** or **To wonder**.

ii.   (To take something seriously, to make it an issue)

Examples:
- *I feel we should let him off this time, but*
  my partners want to ***make*** *something* ***of*** *it.*
- *You're getting too carried away. If I were you, I wouldn't*
  make *too much* ***of*** *the stuff he comes out with.*

Compare with **To make a meal of** (see Page 145).

To strike someone that (To realise, to occur to someone – often suddenly)

Examples:
- *It only* ***struck me*** *this morning* ***that*** *we haven't*
  got round to working out our overheads for the year.
- *Has it ever* ***struck you that*** *she picks him up*
  on every little thing he says?

Note the paradigm of **To strike** is **strike – struck – struck**. Also note the expression To dawn on which can be used in a similar way, but is probably more gradual,
      e.g.   *It's only just* ***dawned on*** *me that we could increase our turnover by talking the Managing Director into taking an early retirement.*

In the pipeline (Plans, ideas, changes which are on the way/being prepared)

Examples:
- *I'm not bothered whether it comes off or not;*
  we've got plenty of alternative schemes **in the pipeline**.
- *We urge shareholders to take up their preference shares and*
  assure everyone that further developments are **in the pipeline**.

To pave the way (To take the first step and therefore make the way ahead easier for other people/things)

Examples:
- *She was the first woman to bring about a change*
  in the role of women in the Church and **paved the way**
  for others like her to go on and achieve similar success.
- *The agreement reached between the two Presidents has*
  paved the way *for a break-through in East/West relations.*

Lesson Three

Feasible (Possible, practical)

Examples:
- *It's just about **feasible** that we'll be able to get things underway by the spring.*
- *Even though it sounds straightforward, you must own up to the fact that, in practice, it's not really **feasible**.**

* i.e. not a very good idea, unrealistic.

Patronising, to patronise (Condescending, to treat someone as if they were a child or unintelligent)

Examples:
- *I find his constant put-downs rather **patronising**.*
- A: *I suppose I might as well go through it all over again, as you didn't catch on the first time.*
  B: *How dare you **patronise** me like that!*

To put on

i.   (To gain in weight)

Example:
- *I can't get over how much weight she has **put on** since her marriage broke up.*

ii.   (To play a record, cassette, etc.)

Example:
- *Can you **put** that Brazilian tape **on** again? I've really taken to Samba.*

iii.   (To turn on*, boil, to begin to cook a meal)

Examples:
- ***Put** the kettle **on**! I could murder a cup of tea.*
- *It's just as well I hadn't **put** the dinner **on**; it would have been ruined.*

* See Page 160.

iv.   (To arrange, to show a play, TV programme, exhibition etc., to transmit)

Examples:
- *We'd like to **put on** a couple of Shakespeare's plays next year but, for the time being, the public will have to make do with some of my own work.*
- *They're **putting on** a series of Japanese films and programmes on BBC1 in the summer; it looks like I'll be watching quite a bit of TV.*

v.   (To pretend – often concerned with illness/injury or one's way of speaking)

Examples:
- A: *You're not accusing me of **putting it*** **on**, are you?*
  B: *No, but I do think you sometimes talk yourself into being ill.*
- A: *I really am feeling under the weather today. I'll never be able to get through this work by 5.30.*
  B: *Stop **putting it*** **on** and get on with it!*
- *When it comes to **putting on** a posh English accent, there's nobody like Tim.*

Note that it is *not* possible to say *He puts on **that** he is ill.* One would have to use **To make out** instead (see Page 71).
* When referring to illness, **on** is usually preceded by the pronoun *it*.

vi.   (To provide an extra service – often transport)

Example:
- *British Rail have been called upon to **put on** more trains during the Christmas period.*

Slump, to slump (A period of economic recession, a decline of standards, position, to fall in price, value or demand)

Examples:
- *The **slump** in trade between the two countries has brought about a mutual decline in tourism.*
- *His patchy form led to the **slump** in his team's fortunes.*
- *Businessmen still haven't come to terms with the fact that the property market has **slumped**.*

See also **To plummet** (Page 149).

To sort out

i. (To put in order, organise, to choose which things should be kept)

Examples:
- *It has just struck me that we've still got to **sort out** all this correspondence.*
- *You won't get on in this world unless you **sort** yourself **out** now.*
- *After you've turned out those drawers, do you think you could **sort out*** which papers are worth keeping?*

Note the noun Sort-out (Colloquial),
  e.g. *This office could do with a good **sort-out**.*
* See also **To go through** (Page 128).

ii. (To solve, work out*, deal with a problem)

Examples:
- *It's a good job we **sorted out** these problems before Christmas; we would never have been able to cope with them otherwise.*
- *If I come unstuck, will you help me **sort out** the hassle with the bank?*

* See Page 26.

Not to be sneezed/sniffed at (Something which deserves consideration and appreciation and should not be ignored, e.g. an achievement, an amount of money received)

Examples:
- *I agree, the profit we made last year in normal circumstances would be nothing to write home about; but on the other hand, it **shouldn't be sneezed at*** during a slump like we're in now.*
- *I don't know why other players put him down. He's already scored twenty goals this season and that's **not to be sniffed at**.*

* i.e. *It's not so bad.*

To fit in

i. (To have something in common with, to feel comfortable with a particular group of people)

Examples:
- *She's very odd; she doesn't actually **fit in** with anyone.*
- *Don't get me wrong: I'd love to come round but I don't really **fit in*** (with your workmates).*

See also **To fit** (Page 69).
* i.e. *I feel the odd one out* (see Page 85).

ii. (To suit, agree with, e.g. someone's plans or ideas conforming to another person's)

Examples:
- *I'm dreading this take-over; their schemes don't **fit in** with what I had planned for the company.*
- *It's not worth falling out with them, just because their holiday plans don't **fit in** with ours.*

iii. (To find the time to do something, see/deal with someone)

Examples:
- A: *Would you mind handling this matter?*
  B: *I'm sorry, I'm off to Spain tomorrow and I don't think I'll be able to **fit** it **in**.*
- *Can't the doctor **fit** me **in** tomorrow morning? I've got so many things to sort out in the afternoon.*

iv. (To have enough room, space, to accommodate)

Example:
- *I haven't got a clue how we're going to **fit** everyone **in**. We'll just have to make the most of my parents' living room.*

Note *To squeeze in* can also be used for this meaning and **iii.** above.

To go to one's head

i.   (To get excited, carried away*, show off because of one's success)

Examples:
- *Winning the championship has just sunk in,*
  but I won't let it **go to my head**.
- *He makes out that he takes everything in his stride, but*
  it's quite apparent that his promotion has **gone** *(straight)* **to his head**.

* See Page 106.

ii.   (To make someone drunk quickly – usually a small amount of alcohol)

Example:
- *I love wine; the only drawback is that just*
  one glass **goes** *(straight)* **to my head**.

To stand out

i.   (To be noticed as being much better or more beautiful than the others)

Examples:
- *Out of all the candidates that stood for the Presidency,*
  she **stood out** *as being far and away* the best.*
- *I know I keep going on about it, but*
  you have to admit she **stands out** *in a crowd.°*

* i.e. *easily, without doubt.*
° This does not necessarily mean the person is standing amongst a crowd of people. It is merely an alternative way of saying that someone is strikingly attractive.

ii.   (To be noticed as being different from or more important than other things, to be easily noticed)

Examples:
- *We don't really want colours that will* **stand out**;
  everything must fit in with the natural surroundings.
- *Of all the matters that came up in that meeting,*
  one thing has **stood out** *in my mind and that is, we're not*
  going to get through next year without making some ruthless decisions.
- A: *We're bound to get lost.*
  B: *Nonsense! I gather that all the signs*
  to the village **stand out** *clearly.*

Note the colloquial expression To stand out a mile which means very clear or obvious,
     e.g.   *I can't believe you never caught on to the fact that she fancied you; it* **stands out a mile**!

To stand out against (To oppose something strongly, to protest against – often in a political sense)

Example:
- *The party's success in the elections has been overshadowed by the fact that many members intend to **stand out against** the proposals which are currently in the pipeline.*

Menial (Monotonous and requiring very little skill or intelligence – usually a job or piece of work)

Examples:
- *As Managing Director, you can't afford the time to take on these **menial** tasks; get one of the youngsters round to give you a hand.*
- *He's not really on the ball enough to handle these clients. Can't we give him something more **menial** to do?*

*"She's very odd; she doesn't actually **fit in** with anyone."*

(see page 174)

PETER'S DIARY:

21st September

Today it really *dawned* on me that I don't *fit in* with the rest of my class. We were asked to *sort out* our desks, and it *stood out a mile* that mine was the messiest. I've just never *got round to* tidying it up. John was told that he was the neatest person in the class. This *went to his head* and now he's showing off that he knows how to *get round* the teacher, Mr. Brown. When the teacher inspected my desk, he gave me a *patronising* look as if to say "How old are you? Don't you have any self respect?" Whenever he's in a bad mood, it's always me that he *takes it out on* but I just *take it in my stride*; I'm used to it now.

When I got home, Mum asked me what I *made of* her new-style cheesecake. I *dithered* a little before giving her an answer. It didn't *stand out* as being different from any of the others – in fact I didn't think it was *anything to write home about* at all. However, I didn't tell her that of course, although I hinted that it *didn't come up to scratch*, when I asked her when she was going to make her old-style cheesecake again.

25th September

Today, our team, Stockton United, had a football match against Rockford Rovers, our rival team from the next village. Last time we played them, we lost 10 – 0 but this time we had a couple of new players, and it was *feasible* that we could at least put up a fight. However, we *came off* rather badly and this time we lost 12 – 2. Our captain tried to *put it down to* bad luck, saying "We got two goals, and that's *not to be sniffed at!*" The manager, on the other hand, really *turned on* us, saying "It never *struck* me how bad you were until today! I've got a few ideas *in the pipeline* which are going to revolutionise this team and *pave the way* for future boys to be proud to *put on* a Stockton United shirt. We're starting *from scratch*. That's the best way of *sorting out* this team's problems." I suppose he is right. To tell the truth, we're *not a patch on* the team we used to be, but that may be because we've all *put on* so much weight. This is one of the *drawbacks* of growing up.

CLIENT: *Good morning, Howard.*

LAWYER: *Hello Richard. How are things?*

CLIENT: *At home everything's fine but in the office it's all upside down.*

LAWYER: *Oh, how come?*

CLIENT: *Well, basically, I've fallen out with my partners.*

LAWYER: *Over anything in particular?*

CLIENT: *Well yes, quite a few things actually.*

LAWYER: *Just before you continue ... Lisa can you put the kettle on, I'm sure Howard would like a cup of tea.*

CLIENT: *Oh thank you, I'd love one. Anyway, the first thing is we've all had to fork out for this new computer system we've had installed, and I wasn't even consulted. I think we could easily have made do with the old one. Secondly, their plans for the future of the company don't fit in with mine at all. I think that during the slump in property prices, we should be making alternative investments. Not one of the schemes that they thought of has come off and their excuses are always the same, i.e. "We're going through a bad patch".*

LAWYER: *And what's your turnover been like this year?*

CLIENT: *I can't tell you off the top of my head but I know it's nothing to write home about. You see, I never get to see the accounts. I'm only given menial tasks to carry out and if I ask to do something else, I'm told that I'm always trying to get my own way. However, the worst thing I have to put up with is that at least two of my partners, John and Trevor, are always putting me down in front of the staff. I won't stand for that any longer.*

LAWYER: *So you want to split from the partnership?*

CLIENT: *Yes, most of us do.*

LAWYER: *Well, I'll have to go through your Partnership Agreement to see what you can get out of it but I can tell you that there is a new Partnership Act which will be difficult to get round.*

CLIENT: *Can't we just divide everything equally?*

178

LAWYER: *That may not be feasible. It will turn on the Partnership Agreement and the way it has been interpreted. Do you think there's any possibility of patching everything up?*

CLIENT: *Not as far as I'm concerned. However, the Senior Partner, Peter Smith, has sat on the fence throughout this issue and he doesn't want to make anything out of the rows we've been having.*

LAWYER: *Right, OK. I think we've gone as far as we can today. How about next week? I can probably fit you in on Tuesday at 11:00am.*

CLIENT: *Let me put that down in my diary.*

Chapter Eight: **Exercise**

CHOOSE THE CORRECT WORD FROM THOSE IN BLUE
Answers on page 206.

A CONVERSATION BETWEEN A PRIEST AND A MEMBER OF HIS CONGREGATION:

WOMAN: *Hello, Father O'Leary.*

PRIEST: *Good morning, Doreen. What can I do for you?*

WOMAN: *Well, it's difficult to know where to start.*

PRIEST: *Take your time; we're not in a hurry.*

WOMAN: *I've so many problems which need [1](solving/tidying/sort/sorting) out. I wanted to come and see you some weeks ago but unfortunately, I didn't get [2](through/across/round/over) to it. Firstly, it's my marriage; we've been going through a bad [3](patch/year/month/disadvantage) recently and even though we haven't [4](got/fallen/broken/taken) out with each other, it [5](tells/speaks/stands/is) out a [6](mile/far/distance/noticeable) that something is missing in our marriage.*

PRIEST: *What do you think it can be put [7](up/down/off/on) to?*

WOMAN: *It's very difficult to say. You see, on the question of getting married, we didn't exactly [8](run/walk/go/dither) around.*

PRIEST: *How do you mean?*

WOMAN: *Well, we'd only been seeing each other for a month when Peter suggested we get married. I didn't really [9](suit/make/go/fit) in with his friends but apart from that, I couldn't see any other [10](drawbacks/advantages/gimmicks/faults). On the looks side, Peter is nothing to [11](bring/shout/write/talk) home [12](of/about/at/from), but I was attracted to the way he took life in his [13](way/walk/nature/stride). It struck me that he was the type that always [14](got/took/claimed/managed) his own [15](stride/way/back/method) like a little child and that appealed to me. Now, unfortunately, everything seems to have changed.*

PRIEST: *In what way?*

WOMAN: *In many ways. Very soon after we got married, he started [16](criticising/taking/putting/encouraging) me down in front of his friends. He would tell them that I was spending all of his money, [17](spending/wasting/forking/splashing) out on clothes and expensive dresses which didn't fit me anyway, because I was putting [18](off/down/up/on) so much weight.*

PRIEST: *How nasty!*

WOMAN: *Oh, that's nothing! He would also tell them that I didn't turn him [19](on/up/down/around) and that he wanted a woman who would [20](show/make/stand/look) out in a [21](group/crowd/audience/gathering). This was all before he started drinking. You see, Father, even the slightest drop of alcohol goes [22](immediately/directly/straight/always) to his [23](feet/head/nose/mouth). His [24](good/unnecessary/sensible/patronising) behaviour I can put up with, but not his drunkenness. Please don't tell anyone else; I don't want this to get [25](off/over/through/round).*

PRIEST: *Of course not. But why do you think he turned to alcohol?*

WOMAN: *He had problems with his business for quite a while. A few deals which he had planned for this year didn't [26](go/come/break/turn) off. On top of that, his [27](expense/money/expensive/overheads) have almost doubled in recent years. I could understand it if he was simply [28](bringing/making/driving/taking) his business worries out on me, but it seems to me more than that. I think it has finally [29](struck/opened/dawned/realised) on both of us that we need to start our lives from [30](today/scratch/now/beginning)... without each other.*

PRIEST: *Well that's very honest of you to admit that, but are you sure that it's not possible to [31](make/put/tie/patch) up your differences? Perhaps your husband would like to come and talk with me as well. What do you make [32](out/up/of/from) that idea?*

WOMAN: *Well, I could try to persuade him, but he'll probably come up with some excuse, like he hasn't got the time to [33](push/fit/bring/suit) it in or that reconciliation isn't a [34](good/feasible/probable/suitable) prospect.*

PRIEST: *Well, we don't know until we give it a go. Let's try to fix a time which is suitable for all of us. How about next month?*

WOMAN: *Well, [35](off/of/from/at) the top of my [36](chest/head/hands/tongue) I don't know exactly what I have planned and of course, I can't answer for my husband. Can I give you a call later on this evening?*

PRIEST: *Of course you can. I'll speak to you later on then. Bye for now.*

I must admit that I was a bit put out having to [37](*look/splash/fork/spend*) *out £9 for a cinema ticket but I soon forgot about it once the film got underway. This was the second Brian Smith film which they had put* [38](*on/off/up/down*) *at The Lumiere this year. In recent years, he has had four nominations as Best Director... something not to be* [39](*proud/ignored/ashamed/sniffed*) *at. However, this film was, at best,* [40](*fussy/messy/patchy/dodgy*). *Susan Rogers and David Cunningham are fine in the leading roles but, surprisingly enough, it's the script that doesn't* [41](*come/go/make/tie*) *up to* [42](*average/now/scratch/itch*). *It is much too predictable and fails to* [43](*fit/go/suit/buy*) *in with the period in which the film is set. It's about a family's struggle to survive in America during the economic* [44](*days/boom/slump/period*) *of the 1930s. A small town in the South decides to stand out* [45](*for/about/against/besides*) *the Government which* [46](*breaks/puts/pushes/crashes*) *down the rebellion with force. Even the local police turn* [47](*on/up/to/of*) *members of the public, most of whom* [48](*go/push/come/take*) *off rather badly. Cunningham and Rogers are married with two small children and they come to the conclusion there is no future for them in the town. They embark on a long journey stretching right across the States, where they encounter many weird and wonderful things. There's not very much to grab one's attention, but the scenery is beautiful. Go and see this film if you've nothing better to do, but I hope Brian Smith has something more exciting in the* [49](*away/place/pipeline/future*).

Lesson One

To get a move on (To hurry up, to get on with*) **Colloquial**

Examples:
- *I think it's about time we **got a move on**; it's getting on for 11 o'clock.*
- *Stop dithering and **get a move on**, otherwise it'll be too late to put yourself down for the competition.*

* See Page 106.

Thick-skinned (Not easily offended or upset)

Example:
- *She's far too **thick-skinned** to take in all the nasty comments that people have been coming out with.*

Blunt

i.   (Not sharp)

Example:
- *You'd be better off using the **blunt** edge of a knife to open this bottle than one of those useless gimmicks.*

ii.   (Frank, straightforward* without trying to be polite)

Examples:
- *Sorry to be **blunt**, but your work is just not up to scratch.*
- *To put° it **bluntly**, I don't fancy your chances of attracting a girl who stands out as much as she does.*

* See Page 58.

° Note this use of To put simply means **to say**. How can I put it? is very often employed when there is a pause in a conversation and the speaker wants to ask himself aloud how he can express something in a better way. He is not expecting an answer from the person he is speaking to,

     e.g.   *Well... **How can I put it?**... It's just not working out...*

To go for

i.   (To attack someone physically or verbally) **Colloquial**

Examples:
- *I only **went for** her last night because there*
was no-one else I could take out my anger on.
- *The dog will **go for** you if you keep winding him up like that.*

Compare with **To turn on**. See Page 160.

ii.   (To fancy,* like, to be attracted to something/someone) **Colloquial**

Examples:
- *I don't generally° **go for** older men, but he really turns me on.*
- *We thoroughly enjoyed the concert; mind you,*
*it's not the type of music we usually° **go for**.*

* See Page 102.
° This use of **To go for** is often used with **generally**, **usually**, **the type**.

iii.   (To apply *for*, to try to get – generally a job, position, etc.)

Examples:
- *I know the odds are against me but*
*I might as well **go for** both universities.*
- *The job as Chief Systems Engineer in this company is*
*so highly sought-after that it's hardly worth **going for**.*

iv.   (To make a choice, to make up one's mind to do something –
often after a period of hesitation/consideration) **Colloquial**

Example:
- *Instead of messing around,*
*why don't you **go for** the one you like the best?*

v.   (To go out to eat, drink, etc.) **Colloquial**

Examples:
- A: *Do you fancy **going for** an Italian tonight?**
- B: *Oh yes, I could really murder a pizza.*
- *Let's **go for** a pint° and get this dreadful day out of our minds.*

* Note the difference between *I fancy **going for** an Italian tonight* and, after reading the menu at the restaurant saying, *I'm going **to go for** the lasagna*, i.e. to choose. (See **iv.** above.)
° Note that a pint is a British measurement of liquid (0.568 litres) but if the liquid is unspecified it is presumed to be **beer**.

184

vi. (To apply *to* – a written or spoken statement which is also applicable to another person/other people)

Examples:
- *I know I'm being rather blunt but what I'm saying*
  ***goes for** everyone in this company, including all the Directors.*
- *Don't you dare make fun of her again, and that **goes for** you too, John!*

To go in for (To take part in/enter a competition, to like doing a particular activity)

Examples:
- *I can't really be bothered, but why don't you*
  ***go in for** the race? You're bound to win it.*
- *My wife will attend any demonstration which stands out against*
  *cruelty to animals, but I don't generally **go in for*** that sort of thing.*

* Compare with **To go for**, meaning to like (see Page 184, **ii.**).

To have a lot/much going for it, him, you, etc. (To have many qualities, advantages)

Examples:
- *I don't know why you keep putting yourself down;*
  ***you've got so much going for you**.*
- *I agree that London is dirty and depressing at times but*
  *when it comes down to it, **it's got a lot going for it**.*

Lethal (Extremely dangerous, capable of killing)

Examples:
- *The police have called on youngsters to hand in*
  *all their **lethal** weapons without fear of prosecution.*
- Tennis:
  His ground strokes are nothing to write home about but
  *he does have a **lethal** serve.*

To get at

i.   (To criticise, have a go at someone*) **Colloquial**

Examples:
- *I'm not trying to get at <u>you</u> in particular;*
  *what I've said **goes for** all those who were involved.*
- *Can't you pick on someone else for a change?*
  *You're always **getting at** me.*

* See Page 68.

ii.   (To suggest indirectly, to try to say, to hint at* –
generally used to express anger or annoyance)

Examples:
- *I don't know what* you're **getting at**, but*
  I'd prefer you to be blunt and tell me what you really think.
- *What° are you **getting at**? I've never even met your wife,*
  let alone asked her round for dinner.

* See Page 38.
° This meaning of **To get at** is generally used with **what**.

iii.   (To reach, find, to get to*)

Examples:
- *I realise it's a hassle, but you'll have to put it*
  *on the top shelf where the dog can't **get at** it.*
- *They are looking into the matter, but it'll*
  *take them quite a while to **get at** the truth.*

* See Page 38.

An eye-opener (A surprising discovery which allows one to realise/understand something in greater detail, a revelation)

Examples:
- *His letters were a real **eye-opener** for me.*
  It had never struck me before how witty* he was.
- *That documentary was an **eye-opener***
  to the goings-on° behind Parliament's doors.

* A witty person is someone who is funny (amusing) and clever in their use of language.
° i.e. *what goes on.* See Page 17.

A rip-off/to rip off*
A con/to con°
A swindle/to swindle
To do†

(A place which charges too much money, an object which is too expensive for its true value, to charge someone much more for something than it is really worth) **Slang**

Examples:
- A: *What do you make of their new restaurant?*

  B: *I reckon it's a **rip-off/a con/a swindle**.*
- *Many of these video games for children are a **rip-off/a con/ a swindle**; the toy shops have got a lot to answer for these days.*
- *£50? I got hold of the same shirt for £20.*
  *You've been **ripped off/conned/swindled/done**!*

* To rip-off also means to copy someone else's work,

  e.g.   *I don't rate him at all. He's simply **ripped off** the 18th century composers.*

° Note the expression To con someone into something which is used in a more general sense of the verb to deceive, to trick, not necessarily involving money.

  e.g.   1.   *He **conned** her **into** thinking that he would put her up for two weeks but he was only having her on.*

  2.   *Many people are **conned into** believing that they can sort out their problems in this way, but I am not so easily taken in.*

Also note that **To con**, **swindle**, **To do** can be used with *out of* + money.

  e.g.   *The fact that she didn't offer him the money, but was* **conned/done/swindled out of** *it, was quite an eye-opener.*

Finally, note that a Con-man/Swindler is someone who **cons/swindles** people.

† Note that there is no noun for **To do** in this sense.

To stand by

i.   (To be a loyal friend, companion to a person who may be very ill or in serious trouble)

Examples:
- *I would never have got over my illness, had* my wife not **stood by** me throughout.*
- *Don't worry, if you own up to the crime, I'll still **stand by**° you.*

* Note that **had** can often be used to mean **if...had** when used in the past conditional. I.e. instead of *I would never have got over my illness, if my wife **had** not stood by me throughout.*

° Compare with **To stick up for** (see Page 109).

ii. (Not to change one's mind about/to stick to* an earlier promise/decision)

Examples:
- I might have known he wouldn't **stand by** his word.
- We will **stand by** what we decided yesterday, unless someone can come up with a better proposal.

* See Page 35.

iii. (Not to take any action to stop something bad happening)

Examples:
- Are you just going to **stand by** and* let him get away with it?
- Most of the crowd who turned out for the protest march **stood by** and* watched as the police turned on some of their members.

* Note that this meaning of **To stand by** is often followed by **and** plus a verb.

iv. (To be ready to help or take action if required)

Examples:
- In case the ambulance drivers don't call off their strike, troops are **standing by**/**on standby*** to take over.
- Even young children **stood by**/were **on standby*** to give the firemen a hand in putting out the fire.

* Note the adjective Standby, used for this meaning only. A *standby* ticket is one used for an aeroplane, theatre, etc. and is bought on the day of the flight or performance at a cheaper rate because it has been returned or not sold.

In the long run (In the end, eventually, after a long period of time – referring to a time in the future)

Examples:
- It may seem uncalled for now but it is paving the way for a secure future and, **in the long run**, you won't regret it.
- I know it sounds like it's a rip-off but **in the long run**, it'll work out to be very economical.

Lesson Two

To entail (To involve, signify)

Examples:
- *You can't afford to get carried away by your promotion until you know what it **entails**.*
- *Starting a new business **entails** much more than putting up the odd £1,000.*

To get down to (To start something which requires concentration and organisation – e.g. a piece of work, a business deal)

Examples:
- *I've been messed about by so many people today. It was getting on for 5 o'clock before I seriously **got down to** work.*
- *I apologise, gentlemen, but we'll have to make do with the small conference room, if we want to **get down to** business this morning.*

To take down (To write, note down something which has been said, dictated)

Examples:
- *It's unheard of for her not to **take down** what the teacher says. What's come over her?*
- *Boss to secretary:*
  *Can you please **take** this letter **down** and then get it off before the last post?*

Compare with **To put down** (see Page 161) which has a wider meaning (i.e. the words do not have to be spoken, they could simply be ideas).

(On the) spur of the moment (At that moment, without hesitation/ consideration, an action/decision which is taken suddenly without previous planning)

Examples:
- *We knew that in the long run there would be more contracts in the pipeline but were forced to go through with the deal **on the spur of the moment**.*
- *A: Did she drop him any hints that she was going to hand in her notice?*
  *B: No, it was just a **spur-of-the-moment** decision.*

(On the) spur of the moment is very similar to **Out of the blue** (see Page 34) except that the former expression generally relates to an action performed *on impulse,* whilst the latter is more concerned with something happening *unexpectedly.*

To drift

i. (To be transported slowly by the movement of water or wind, to float, e.g. an object such as a boat, piece of wood etc.)

Examples:
- *Can you spot that little boat **drifting** (in) towards us?*
- *Weather forecast:*
  *There will be patchy fog **drifting** across the country throughout the day.*

ii. (To move from place to place with no sense of purpose or permanence, at irregular intervals, to move slowly away from a place where people have gathered)

Examples:
- *I don't know what he's up to;*
  *he's been **drifting** in and out of the office all day.*
- *This massive crowd, which has turned out to see*
  *the Queen off, is just beginning to **drift** away.*

iii. (To keep changing the subject, jobs, partners, etc.)

Examples:
- *I wish he would stick to the subject and stop **drifting**.*
- *You'll never get on in life if you keep **drifting** from job to job.**
- *If you ask me, he's a bit of a dodgy character;*
  *he just **drifts** from one relationship to another.°*

To drift off means the same as **To drop off** (see Page 100) but it can also be used to mean **To lose concentration**,

e.g.   *Sorry, I **drifted off** for a second. Would you mind running through it again?*

* A Drifter is a person who **drifts** from place to place, job to job, etc.,

e.g.   *To be blunt, we can't afford to take on **drifters** in this firm.*

° Note that To drift *apart* is used when friends or partners in a relationship become more distant over a period of time,

e.g.   *We didn't really fall out with each other; it's just that, as we grew up, we **drifted apart**.*

Drift

i. (The basic meaning, concept of what someone says)

Examples:
- *From what I can gather, the **drift** of his argument was that the local councils are getting away with murder.*
- *I couldn't quite catch his **drift**. What was he getting at?*

ii. (A gradual development, trend, inclination, change or movement of a particular group of people in a certain direction)

Examples:
- *Interest in package holidays has dropped off in recent years because there has been a general **drift** towards self-catering apartments.*
- *The **drift** of English professors across the Atlantic can be put down to the British Government's reluctance to come up with suitable sponsorships.**

* i.e. *Many English professors are going to America because they are not financially supported by the British Government.*

Cutback, to cutback (A reduction, especially in expenditure, staff, safety, etc., to reduce)

Examples:
- *The staff reluctantly accepted that there would have to be a **cutback** on perks* this year.*
- *This Christmas is bound to be a flop for many high street stores because most people are **cutting back**.°*
- *Quite a number of people are reckoned to have stood out against the **cutbacks**.†*

Compare **To cut back** with **To cut down** (see Page 59). They are very similar in meaning, but **To cut back** is generally preferred when referring to expenditure. Also note that there is *no* noun **Cut-down**.
* A Perk is any benefit which an employee receives apart from his salary, e.g. a car, free medical insurance, etc.
° i.e. *saving money.*
† **Cutbacks** here could refer either to a reduction of staff or of funds.

Borderline (Doubtful, only just acceptable – generally used to describe a person, e.g. exam candidate)

Examples:
- *She'll get through her exams without any trouble, but her brother is more of a **borderline** case.*
- *His mother fancies his chances of getting into Cambridge next year, but I reckon he's rather **borderline**.**

To take everything/what someone says with a pinch of salt (Not to take someone seriously, not to believe everything someone says)

Examples:
- *He comes out with such a lot of rubbish;*
  if I were you, I'd **take everything he says with a pinch of salt**.
- *I warned you to* **take what she says with a pinch of salt**,
  but you fell for her charm; it serves you right!

To wipe out

i.   (To put an end to/get rid of something – often illegal or considered to be unpleasant, and which many people have suffered from or practised)

Examples:
- *What do you make of the council's*
  ambitions to **wipe out** *poverty in the area?*
- *Their attempts to* **wipe out** *racism should not be sneezed at.*

Note To stamp out can also be used in this sense.
Compare with **To crack/clamp down on** (see Page 126). **To wipe out** is stronger in that it means to eliminate completely, whilst **To crack/clamp down on** is merely to take severe action against.

ii.   (To destroy groups of people or other living things)

Examples:
- *The soldiers put up a brave fight but the entire*
  battalion was **wiped out** *by superior enemy forces.*
- *We ought to make the most of the country's wildlife while it is still here.*
  It'll all be **wiped out** *soon, if the more ruthless property developers*
  get their own way.

iii.   (To erase a period of time from memory, to erase, to record over a cassette/video)

Examples:
- *We've been drifting apart for quite a while, but*
  one can't **wipe out** *ten years of marriage just like that.*
- *My dad flew off the handle, when it dawned on him that*
  my mother had **wiped out** *all the films he had recorded.*

To fill in

i.   (To complete a form)

Example:
- *I could do with some help in **filling in** this application form; I don't know what to put down.*

Note the expression *To fill in time* which means to pass the time doing something whilst waiting for something more important to happen (See **To get on with**; Page 106),

e.g.   *I'm fed up with messing around, trying to **fill in time**; I want to get down to business.*

ii.   (To give someone specific information, details – i.e. to fill someone in *on**)
something)

Examples:
- *Could you get back to me sometime before tomorrow and **fill** me **in** on what's going on?*
- *Don't rely on him to **fill** you **in** on anything; he hasn't got a clue.*

* Do not confuse *To fill someone in **on** something* with *To fill in for someone* which means to take over someone's job because that person is not available,

e.g.   *As you really put yourself out for me last week, I'd be delighted to **fill in for you** today if you want to take the day off.*

*"If I were you, I'd **take everything he says with a pinch of salt**."*

(see Page 192)

Lesson Three

One-off (Something which is unlikely to be repeated, unique)

Examples:
- We won't stand for this appalling behaviour. Let's just put it down to poor judgement, and hope that it was a **one-off** incident.
- It's a **one-off** opportunity to get our own back on him. Don't mess it up this time!

To stand up

i. (To be credible/acceptable in a court of law)

Example:
- I know you feel hard-done-by, but your account of what went on will never **stand up** in court.* The jury will just crack up laughing.

* **To stand up** is used for a claim, explanation or a story, rather than a person or thing and is usually followed by *in court*.

ii. (Not to turn up* to a date with someone – i.e. to stand *someone* up)
Colloquial

Examples:
- That's the second time in a row that she was meant to meet me outside the station and she **stood** me **up** again; I can't be bothered with her any more.
- Look at that poor bloke waiting in the rain getting drenched! I bet he's been **stood** up **by** someone.

To stand *someone* up is not used for formal appointments, but generally when a man and woman have arranged to meet each other socially.

* See Page 15.

To stand up to

    i.   (To bear, cope with*)

        Examples:
- *I don't reckon this car will **stand up to** another journey like that one.*
- *Experts say that, in the long run, the economy°*
  *will not be able to **stand up to** excessive borrowing.*

* See Page 12.
° The subject is not generally a person but an object or something more abstract (e.g. *the economy*).

    ii.   (To defend *oneself* verbally against someone more powerful or senior)

        Examples:
- ***Standing up to** the directors entails*
  a lot more guts than you can imagine.
- *At first, she didn't know how to get round her boss but eventually she*
  *found that she could get her own way, simply by **standing up to** him.*

Note that **To stand up *to* someone** is different from To stand up for someone which is the same as **To stick up for someone** (see Page 109), i.e. to defend someone or an idea,

    e.g.   1.   *As he has stood by me throughout this tricky patch,*
                 *I feel obliged to **stand up for him** when he's being picked on.*
            2.   *I've been told that I get too carried away but I believe in **standing up for one**'s rights.*

Take-off/to take off

    i.   (Leaving/to leave the ground in an aeroplane)

        Examples:
- Pilot to cabin crew:
  *Standby for **take-off**!*
- *Do you think we'll be able to **take off***
  in these dodgy weather conditions?

    ii.   (To be successful very quickly, to catch on*)

        Examples:
- *The business really **took off** last summer, but*
  interest began to drop off by October.
- *I don't think those gimmicks will **take off** here.*
  People are fed up with being ripped-off.

This meaning of **To take off** is not generally used for a person (i.e. one *cannot* say *She took off in her career* but *Her career took off*).

To take off should be compared with **To pick up**, which means to improve (see Page 74), and **To come off** (see Page 163) which has a very similar meaning but is more generally concerned with ideas or plans being successful.

* See Page 33.

iii. (To deduct money – usually for tax or price)

Examples:
- *I can't remember off the top of my head whether or not tax has already been **taken off**. I'll have to get the accountant round to fill us in.*
- *Customer to shop assistant:*
  *I've just tried on this shirt and have spotted a small hole in the collar. Will you **take** something **off** for it?*

iv. (To impersonate, imitate someone in order to amuse people) **Colloquial**

Example:
- *I wish you could have seen him **taking off** the boss; we were in hysterics.*

To drop out (To cease being a member or taking part in something, either after or just before it starts – e.g. a course, college, etc.)

Examples:
- *So far, fifty people have said they want to go in for the competition but at least a quarter of them are bound to **drop out** before it gets under way.*
- *I might have known she'd **drop out**. She never sees anything through.*

Note that a Drop-out is a person who has *dropped out* of society, i.e. does not work, socialise or conform in any way,

e.g.   *A few **drop-outs** were turned away from the party.*

To steer clear of (To avoid)

Examples:
- *Your remarks didn't go down well with the directors. I'd **steer clear of** them if I were you.*
- *I tell you what: I'm going to **steer clear of** spicy food from now on.*

It is presumed that students will already know that a Steering wheel is used to drive (*to steer*) a motor vehicle or a ship.

Scruffy, Scruff (Very untidy, an untidy person)

Examples:
- *I'm sorry to keep getting at you, but you've got to do something about your **scruffy** appearance.*
- *He only stands out as being smart because the rest of his family are **scruffs**.*

Scruffy is not generally used for a place.

To cotton on (To catch on*, to realise without being told directly)

Examples:
- *I've dropped so many hints that we could all do with a pay rise, but he still hasn't **cottoned on**.*
- *Do you think she'll ever **cotton on** to the fact that he only dropped out of the course, because he wanted to steer clear of her?*

* See Page 33.

Relentless (Endless, intense)

Examples:
- *She gave in her notice on the spur of the moment, because she could no long handle the **relentless** pressure of the job.*
- *Don't get me wrong; I've got a soft spot for your mother, but she does go on **relentlessly**.*

To vouch for (To confirm the truth of something from personal experience)

Examples:
- A: *She told me that he stood by her throughout her illness.*
  B: *Oh yes, I can **vouch for** that.*
- *I'm afraid I can't **vouch for** her cooking. She's never got round to asking me over.*

To pack up

i. (To finish, tidy up and go home – usually from work) **Colloquial**

Examples:
- *Come on, let's call it a day. It's time we **packed up**.*
- *Get a move on! I want to **pack up** by seven o'clock.*

Note the expression To pack in (**colloquial**) which also means to stop doing something, but usually because the person is fed up with what he or she is doing, e.g. a job. It generally has a greater degree of permanence than **To pack up**,

e.g. *Her job is really getting to her now, but if she **packs** it **in**, she'll end up drifting around again.*

Also note the expression Pack it in! which has the same meaning as **Cut it out!** (see Page 59) and is probably preferred in British English,

e.g. ***Pack it in!** Can't you see you're driving us all up the wall.*

ii. (To stop working, to get broken) **Colloquial**

Examples:
- A: *Why don't we go for a drive tomorrow afternoon?*
  B: *That'll be a little tricky; the car's **packed up** again.*
- *Your computer is bound to **pack up** if you use it relentlessly.*

Compare with **To cut out** (see Page 59) which is generally used when something *suddenly* stops working without warning, rather than simply to report the fact that a machine is broken and will not start. **To pack up**, on the other hand, can be used in *either* sense.

*"It's a **one-off** opportunity to get our own back on him. Don't mess it up this time!"*

(see Page 194)

198

TWO OLD FRIENDS WALKING IN THE PARK:

FRED: *Come along,* get a move on!

STAN: *Hang on a minute. Remember, I'm not as young as you. My legs won't* stand up to *much more punishment. Do you know, I've just been thinking about the first time I came to this park. I was about 17 and I was due to meet a pretty young girl called Cynthia at the entrance. She* stood me up!

FRED: *How long did you wait?*

STAN: *Oh, ages. She never turned up, but I was prepared to put it down to a* one-off *incident – maybe I got the time wrong. Anyway, I was willing to give her another chance, so we made a further arrangement. I* packed up *from work at about 5pm and realised that I was looking rather* scruffy, *so I went home and changed. This time, I arranged to meet her in town because she said she fancied* going for *a coffee. What I didn't expect was for her to bring her Alsatian dog with her. I must admit, I was rather stuck for words. She said "I hope you don't mind, but I've brought my dog, Jason, along with me." Wherever I go, he goes." I made no comment but couldn't help noticing that the dog was showing me his* lethal *teeth. Before I had a chance to say hello, he* went for *me and then started barking* relentlessly. *Meanwhile, my date just* stood by *and laughed. I threatened to sue her for owning a dangerous dog and she rather* bluntly *said 'Nothing you say would ever* stand up *in court. You're a fool – it stands out a mile' It's a good job I'm* thick-skinned!

FRED: *And that, I presume, was the end of a beautiful relationship.*

STAN: *Of course, but I could never quite* wipe *her* out *from my memory whenever I came to this park.*

FRED: *I remember* conning *my dad* into *taking me here. I told him that there were beautiful flowers and trees in the park but what I really wanted was for him to help me fly my kite. You see, I thought he could* fill me in *as to what it* entailed. *The kite* took off *like a rocket but then it began to* drift *across the sky like a lonely bird. Then suddenly,* on the spur of the moment, *the kite decided to fly towards the trees, where, of course, it got stuck. My dad looked at me and then the trees, and at me again. I didn't* cotton on. *Then it dawned on me that he was expecting me to climb the tree to release the kite. My dad said he would* stand by *in case I fell. I didn't know whether or not he was joking. I had learned from my mother to* take *everything my dad said* with a pinch of salt, *but this time he was serious. He warned me to* steer clear of *the little branches that would break if I trod on them. I was, to say the least, somewhat daunted by the task I was being forced to take on. I had* dropped out *of physical training classes some time ago and climbing wasn't one of the activities I usually* went in for. *Nevertheless, I had a go.*

FRED: *I* went for *what I reckoned was the easiest route and got to the branch which was holding the kite. I carefully slid myself forward until I reached a position where I thought I could* get at it. *I was wrong! I completely missed the kite, slipped and pulled the branch down. This, fortunately, released the kite. My father* stood by *his word and was ready to catch me but he wasn't prepared to receive the kite, which came crashing down on his head. I cracked up laughing and nearly fell off the tree. The kite was damaged beyond repair and my father realised that coming to the park with his young son had been a real* eye-opener *for him.*

TWO COLLEAGUES AT WORK:

CELIA: *Do you know what, Linda: I just can't seem to* get down to *work today. I've just* taken down *this letter the boss wants me to get off and every time I try to concentrate, I just* drift off.

LINDA: *Maybe you've got something else on your mind!*

CELIA: *What are you* getting at?

LINDA: *Oh, come on, own up! Who is he?*

CELIA: *Well, if you must know, I have met someone, actually. His name's Tony.*

LINDA: *What's he like?*

CELIA: *To be honest he's not the type I usually* go for.

LINDA: *What do you mean?*

CELIA: *He's quite academic and not very business-minded. He works for a charity that aims to* wipe out *starvation in the Third World by the end of the century. He says we must help the poorer countries* stand up to *the exploitation of their land by the West and...*

LINDA: *You're* drifting *again. I don't want to know his politics. Sorry to be* blunt, *but is he good looking?*

CELIA: *Oh yes, certainly! Your friend, Wendy, will* vouch for *that.*

LINDA: *Wendy? When has she met him?*

CELIA: *Well, Tony invited me to the opera last week which meant that I had to leave work early. So I asked Wendy to* fill in for me *for the rest of the day. He came to the office to pick me up and she saw him then.*

LINDA: *I'll have to speak to her then. I'm sure she will* fill me in on *all the interesting details.*

200

CELIA: *Actually, our relationship has really* taken off *in a big way. He's taking me to a French restaurant in the city centre on Saturday.*

LINDA: *Oh, you're bound to get* ripped off *there! Anyway, I would have thought that it would be against his principles to splash out on expensive meals. You know,* in the long run, *I can't see this relationship working at all.*

CELIA: *Oh,* I catch your drift. *You're jealous.*

LINDA: *How can you accuse me of jealousy when I have* stood by *you all these years?*

BOSS: Pack it in, *you two! Doesn't anyone do any work round here?*

*"Sorry to be **blunt**, but your work is just not up to scratch."*

(see Page 183)

Chapter Nine: Exercise

CHOOSE THE CORRECT WORD FROM THOSE IN BLUE
Answers on page 205.

A MAN AND WOMAN VISIT A MARRIAGE COUNSELLOR:

COUNSELLOR: *I'd like to [1](fit/tell/fill/give) you in on what these counselling sessions [2](give/play/entail/take). Firstly, I'm going to listen to both of you expressing your feelings. I don't want either of you to [3](drive/avoid/go/steer) clear of any subject, even if it means you have to be [4](truthful/blunt/sharp/liar). At this early stage, I may occasionally offer advice on the [5](spur/strike/break/light) of the [6](moment/day/minute/exact) but I don't want to go on [7](ever more/relentlessly/ages/endless). You may see me [8](throwing/taking/putting/going) down some notes from time to time, but don't let that put you off. I will be making most of my suggestions much later on in the course. So now, let's get [9](up/through/across/down) to business. Gloria, tell me about your marriage.*

GLORIA: *Well, we've been married for ten years. I'd say that the first seven years were reasonably successful. John's business had [10](taken/come/gone/brought) off in a big way and we agreed that we could now afford to start a family. I fell pregnant and [11](resigned/handed/packed/gave) in my job. I didn't have the easiest of pregnancies.*

JOHN: *Yes, I can [12](confirm/agree/go/vouch) for that.*

GLORIA: *I must say, John [13](walked/stood/went/come) by me throughout. However, it was soon after I gave birth when the problems started. I had post-natal depression and was advised by my doctor to have special classes with other mothers. After two sessions, I [14](went/got/dropped/jumped) out. I couldn't handle them at all. I didn't fit in with the other women and I was told that I was only a [15](unique/borderline/different/individual) case and that in the [16](long/high/short/large) run, I'd be better off resting at home. However, being a mother was a real [17](shocking/surprise/eye-opener/pleasure) for me. I had no idea what I was letting myself in for. John then started to get [18](at/off/on/through) me, saying things like I had nothing [19](standing/going/supporting/bearing) for me as far as motherhood was concerned and that I had become an untidy [20](scruff/clumsy/bossy/choosy). His friends can take what he comes out with with a [21](lot/pinch/punch/glass) of salt, but I am not so [22](thick-skinned/sensitive/highly-strung/stubborn). I tried [23](making/going/dealing/standing) up to him but that made him more aggressive. Whenever we were in company, he would go [24](off/through/at/for) me.*

COUNSELLOR: *In a physical or verbal sense?*

GLORIA: *Oh, only verbally. He has only once tried to hit me, but that was a*
25(only/one-off/friendly/unhappy) incident which we both regretted. No, he would
tell people, for example, that I had 26(taken/pushed/wiped/got) out all of his golfing
videos on purpose or that I had 27(joked/persuaded/encouraged/conned) him into
joining a health club.

JOHN: *What rubbish! As usual, you're just 28(racing/drifting/running/walking) from*
subject to subject without making any sense.

[Turning to the Counsellor]

You know, when I met Gloria for the first time, I told myself "Now that's the type I
29(like/go/fancy/attract) for" but I thought that if I arranged to go out with her, she
would 30(show/turn/give/stand) me up.

COUNSELLOR: *Why were you so lacking in confidence?*

JOHN: *It's just my nature, and also I had gone 31(at/about/for/to) several jobs in the City*
and was turned down by each one; so I wasn't feeling terribly sure of myself.
Nevertheless, I seemed to impress her with my sense of humour. In particular, I
used to be quite good at 32(taking/picking/pushing/making) off famous people.
This made her laugh which, in turn, gave me the courage to ask her out. As Gloria
mentioned, at first we had happy days in each other's company. For instance, we
would go 33(in/out/up/about) for marathons and other competitions together. It
was really great fun. However, over a period of time we began to drift
34(away/apart/off/back). I admit I probably got carried away with my job, but
Gloria became more and more self-centred. She'd take no interest in my work, or
most of the people I met. It seemed as though she wanted to
35(wipe/take/wash/clean) out our first happy years together. A marriage can only
36(bring/go/take/stand) up to a certain amount of pressure, then it collapses.

COUNSELLOR: *Well, I can catch the 37(direction/point/drift/way) of both of your arguments.*
Remember, everything we do in life needs some direction and that
38(goes/makes/speaks/is) for marriage too... We'll have to 39(go/pack/finish/end) up
for today's session but let's pick up where we left off next time.

Answers to Exercises

Chapter One

(1) ages; (2) while; (3) about; (4) turn; (5) books; (6) own; (7) turned; (8) point; (9) better; (10) turned; (11) reluctant; (12) fuss; (13) turnover; (14) handy; (15) better; (16) overdraft; (17) posh; (18) doing; (19) might; (20) bet; (21) fussy; (22) come; (23) afford; (24) gone; (25) handle; (26) goes; (27) going; (28) come; (29) handy; (30) going; (31) make; (32) come; (33) cope; (34) bit; (35) gone; (36) to; (37) going; (38) better; (39) stalemate; (40) gone; (41) afford; (42) getting; (43) back; (44) showing; (45) come; (46) gone; (47) upturn; (48) afford; (49) well; (50) going; (51) day; (52) went; (53) going; (54) handy; (55) might; (56) well.

Chapter Two

(1) bump; (2) stuck; (3) could; (4) with; (5) appalling; (6) work; (7) what; (8) up; (9) take; (10) down; (11) well; (12) apparently; (13) catch; (14) hints; (15) stand; (16) get; (17) wrong; (18) stick; (19) standing; (20) apparent; (21) bound; (22) bossy; (23) clumsy; (24) lands; (25) feet; (26) answer; (27) awkward; (28) all; (29) worked; (30) out; (31) of; (32) breakthrough; (33) up; (34) appearances; (35) stuck; (36) for; (37) felt; (38) to; (39) time; (40) being; (41) catching; (42) dreadful; (43) coming; (44) with; (45) answer; (46) for; (47) nasty; (48) sue.

Chapter Three

(1) filthy; (2) bothered; (3) put; (4) nagging; (5) spotless; (6) put; (7) rewarding; (8) cut; (9) give; (10) notice; (11) sacked; (12) comes; (13) unheard; (14) takes; (15) granted; (16) turned; (17) bring; (18) put; (19) straightforward; (20) fight; (21) frown; (22) breaking; (23) put; (24) advantage; (25) broke; (26) gather; (27) away; (28) put; (29) turned; (30) hold-up; (31) served; (32) told; (33) follow; (34) taken; (35) frowned; (36) upon; (37) bring; (38) straightforward.

Chapter Four

(1) row; (2) go; (3) flew; (4) handle; (5) dodge; (6) hectic; (7) over; (8) made; (9) ball; (10) pick; (11) picked; (12) odds; (13) cross; (14) odds; (15) come; (16) up; (17) make; (18) odd; (19) row; (20) get; (21) murder; (22) off; (23) getting; (24) over; (25) on; (26) have; (27) over; (28) take; (29) over; (30) odd; (31) call; (32) day; (33) pick; (34) off; (35) make; (36) over; (37) pick; (38) off; (39) odd; (40) out; (41) turned; (42) make; (43) round; (44) picked; (45) to; (46) drove; (47) bend; (48) odd; (49) dodgy; (50) rule; (51) make; (52) picking.

Chapter Five

(1) through; (2) dread; (3) got; (4) off; (5) raving; (6) overrated; (7) gullible; (8) taken; (9) mind; (10) daunting; (11) funnily; (12) on; (13) uncalled; (14) along; (15) fancy; (16) chances; (17) wonder; (18) up; (19) shows; (20) through; (21) fancy; (22) look; (23) fun; (24) run; (25) on; (26) carried; (27) hassle; (28) outcome; (29) over; (30) hold; (31) fancied; (32) get; (33) getting; (34) for; (35) murder; (36) dreading; (37) taken; (38) in; (39) stick; (40) biased; (41) fancy; (42) through; (43) get; (44) weather; (45) along.

Chapter Six

(1) up; (2) done; (3) through; (4) terms; (5) out; (6) see; (7) verge; (8) around; (9) along; (10) talk; (11) through; (12) outrageous; (13) get; (14) crack; (15) reckon; (16) cracked; (17) out; (18) just; (19) well; (20) scrapped; (21) laid; (22) ruthless; (23) through; (24) might; (25) known; (26) come; (27) messing; (28) off; (29) talked; (30) seeing; (31) messing; (32) getting; (33) off; (34) up; (35) caters: (36) most; (37) off; (38) come; (39) alone; (40) around; (41) off; (42) grasp.

Chapter Seven

(1) letting; (2) for; (3) run; (4) hang; (5) clue; (6) underwent; (7) brought; (8) wind; (9) plunged; (10) up; (11) pull; (12) strung; (13) wound; (14) meal; (15) grip; (16) spot; (17) rut; (18) down; (19) into; (20) plunge; (21) underway; (22) called; (23) to; (24) pop; (25) into; (26) down; (27) fooled; (28) got; (29) winding; (30) in; (31) run-down; (32) off-chance; (33) caught; (34) put; (35) spot; (36) gimmicks; (37) fall; (38) unwind.

Chapter Eight

(1) sorting; (2) round; (3) patch; (4) fallen; (5) stands; (6) mile; (7) down; (8) dither; (9) fit; (10) drawbacks; (11) write; (12) about; (13) stride; (14) got; (15) way; (16) putting; (17) splashing; (18) on; (19) on; (20) stand; (21) crowd; (22) straight; (23) head; (24) patronising; (25) round; (26) come; (27) overheads; (28) taking; (29) dawned; (30) scratch; (31) patch; (32) of; (33) fit; (34) feasible; (35) off; (36) head; (37) fork; (38) on; (39) sniffed; (40) patchy; (41) come; (42) scratch; (43) fit; (44) slump; (45) against; (46) puts; (47) on; (48) come; (49) pipeline.

Chapter Nine

(1) fill; (2) entail; (3) steer; (4) blunt; (5) spur; (6) moment; (7) relentlessly; (8) taking; (9) down; (10) taken; (11) packed; (12) vouch; (13) stood; (14) dropped; (15) borderline; (16) long; (17) eye-opener; (18) at; (19) going; (20) scruff; (21) pinch; (22) thick-skinned; (23) standing; (24) for; (25) one-off; (26) wiped; (27) conned; (28) drifting; (29) go; (30) stand; (31) for; (32) taking; (33) in; (34) apart; (35) wipe; (36) stand; (37) drift; (38) goes; (39) pack.

Index